THE CULTURAL HISTORY OF THE
ARABS

THE CULTURAL HISTORY OF THE
ARABS

TEXT AND PHOTOGRAPHS
BY HENRI STIERLIN

Cover

This spiral minaret, 55 m (182 ft) high, crowns the great mosque at Samarra (Iraq), built between 848 and 852 by Caliph al-Mutawaqqil.

Endpapers

One of the facades of the octagonal Dome of the Rock in Jerusalem. One of the holy places of Islam, the Dome was built in 687 on the esplanade of the Temple of Solomon, which had first been destroyed by Nebuchadnezzar, then rebuilt by Herod and razed again by Titus in AD 70. Here the marble lower section is in the style of the Byzantine tradition; above, a polychrome ceramic tile decoration from the Ottoman period has replaced an earlier mosaic facing.

Title page

Funerary stele from Palmyra. In this rich gateway to the desert, between the Mediterranean and the Euphrates on the trade route from the Far East, an Arab kingdom emerged to shine brilliantly but briefly during the 3rd century AD. In Palmyra, the Arab tongue combined with Greek and Aramaic writing. (Musée d'Art et d'Histoire, Geneva)

Photo credits

All the 165 colour photographs illustrating this book are the work of Henri Stierlin, with the following exceptions:
Yvan Butler, Geneva, pages 6, 7, 8, 9, 10, 12 bottom, 22, 23 bottom, 24-25, 27.
Alain Saint-Hilaire, Bouffemont, pages 11, 12 top, 13.
Abdelaziz Frikha, Tunis, page 39.
Naud (Ziolo, Paris), page 59 top.
Percheron (Ziolo, Paris), page 59 bottom.
Maurice Babey (Ziolo, Paris), pages 61 left, 71 bottom, 72 bottom, 72-73, 73 bottom.
Maximilien Bruggmann, Yverdon, pages 90, 91, 92, 93, 94, 95.
The author would also like to express his gratitude to the management of the Bagdad Museum, the Mossul Museum, the Top Kapi Library, Istanbul, and the Musée d'Art et d'Histoire, Geneva, for permission to publish photographs of the works in their collections. Finally he would like to thank the authorities in the Arab Republic of Egypt, in Jordan, Syria and Iraq for their help in the preparation of this volume.

Contents

Arabia before Islam

The desert of Saoudi Arabia: the greater part of the Arabian interior is sand desert.

We generally think of the Arabs as emerging out of nothing just after Mohammed's preaching, to erupt into the world of Antiquity, overturn it and annihilate it. All too many works on the Arab world have been produced taking as their starting point this sudden expansion of the Knights of Islam in the 8th century after Christ.

The Arab world did not begin with the Hegira in 622; it was then already a thousand years old. Nor was it swamped by the new religion which sprang from it and which then went on to absorb so many other peoples. Nor indeed was its role a destructive one as so many authors have sought to prove; on the contrary, Arabia gave birth to one of the great civilisations of mankind. It is our aim in this study, through text and image together, to encourage an understanding of the history, now well-established but insufficiently widely known, of this people from one of the most fascinating areas in the Middle East.

Our evocation of the Arab world falls into three major sections. The first includes four chapters, dealing with the pre-Islamic period in the interior of the Arab peninsula and on the peninsula's southern edge; here influences made themselves felt first from Achaemenid Persia and the Hellenistic kingdoms, then later from Rome and Byzantium on the one hand and the Parthians and Sassanians on the other. With Petra, Palmyra and Hatra, those gateways to the desert now known to have been Arab cities, we shall see the first Arab penetration into the world of antiquity.

The second section, embracing three chapters, concerns the age of classical Islam, beginning in the 7th century with the message of the prophet Mohammed and the establishment of the Umayyad Empire, then dealing with the Abbassid empire that followed. From Mecca and Medina in Arabia, the spiritual and political centre of gravity moved during this period to Jerusalem, Damascus, Bagdad and Samarra. These capitals of the caliphs were centres of immense territorial possessions constituting an Islamic world which stretched from the Atlantic to the Indus and from Spain to central Asia.

The third section, which also includes three chapters, deals with the world of Islam in its Arab provinces during the Middle Ages. In fact, from the 10th century on, the immense empire rapidly fragmented following a whole series of "national" reactions, as much in Fatimid Egypt as in Persia and central Asia where the rise of Turkish power was early mapped out. From this medieval period of Islam we shall concentrate on those regions where the language of the Prophet had been definitively established, from Mesopotamia to Morocco. These are the days of confrontation with the crusaders, and of the rise of the Mamluks' power in Egypt, with Cairo, their capital, becoming in its turn the centre of the Arab world and taking on considerable splendour.

Centuries of labour have produced this extraordinary work, the artificial terrassing of the steep mountainsides of the Yemen, making cultivation possible in a country-side that receives seasonal rainfall during the monsoon.

In the rare fertile valleys of the Yemen, competition between tribes for possession of the precious earth led to dwellings being concentrated in high fortified towers.

At the risk of repetition, we should nonetheless underline the fact that this Arab world is not to be confused either with the *Islamic* world nor with the world of Moslem Arabs. The first includes, besides the Arabs, all the Moslem communities of Persia, central Asia, and India, first with the Turkish Seljuks and later the Ottomans and Mongols, and indeed also includes Indonesia and parts of Africa. The second classification is on the other hand too restrictive, as it includes only the Arabs after the Hegira and excludes the early beginnings of their pre-Islamic civilisation and expansion.

At the foot of the Yemeni mountain range, a fortified town on the banks of a wadi, amid sparse vegetation.

Partly abandoned, a typical agglomeration of Yemeni dwellings, with its high defensive towers built in unbaked brick.

Detail of a tower serving as a fortified concentration of dwellings on several floors.

This particular delineation of the Arab world as we have defined it is based on the history of a people who inhabited Arabia from the time of Antiquity and which knew, even before the preaching of Mohammed, a many-faceted culture of some historical importance, and not lacking in grandeur. But it was incontestably the Koran, over a thousand years after the first appearance of a specifically Arab culture, which in the 7th century founded the massive unifying movement from which was born the Arab expansion, carrying the Moslem religion right across the world.

The Arabian Peninsula

Thirteen times the area of Britain, lying at the junction of Asia and Africa, the Arabian peninsula is bordered on three sides by sea: the Persian Gulf to the north-east, the Indian Ocean and the Gulf of Aden to the south, and the Red Sea to the west. Arabia is linked to the continent by the vast deserts of Jordan, Syria and Iraq, and is separated from Egypt by the Sinai peninsula. This vast territory is mostly made up of arid lands. This is particularly true of the deserts of the north and centre, together with the Hijaz, which are the Arabia Petraea and Arabia Deserta of which the Romans speak. The south, on the contrary, has mountains of considerable size along the Red Sea and the Gulf of Aden and in the territory of Oman. These mountain barriers of southern Arabia, particularly in the Yemen, produce a relatively abundant rainfall in the monsoon season. And the generous rain, together with a system of irrigation and terracing all up the sides of the djebels, makes the cultiva-

Facing page:
Far out in the Yemeni desert, at Marib, stand these eight monolithic pillars, remnants of a temple with an oval enclosure, dedicated to a lunar god. The Awwam, with the powerful architecture of these perfectly-dressed 8-metre (24-foot) pillars, must have been the primary South Arabian sanctuary of the 5th century BC.

In a region of southern Arabia which today is entirely desert, many vestiges remain of the civilisation which flourished there in the 5th century BC. These characters in Himyarite script, superbly carved, bear witness to a culture of great originality.

The introduction of the horse into southern Arabian probably dates no further back than the 5th century BC. It was, in any case, later than the use of the camel, or dromedary, which made possible the emergence of caravan traffic at the dawn of the first millenium before Christ.

tion of food crops possible. Besides the date palms of the coastal plains and the oases one finds incense and myrrh trees whose produce has for thousands of years constituted the basic revenue of this Happy Arabia, Arabia Felix.

The Arabs in the interior and the northern deserts of the peninsula were nomadic or semi-nomadic herdsmen, but in the south they were farmers and therefore sedentary. In many areas nomads and farmers co-existed, the nomads living from the trade carried on by their caravans of camels, as well as from their herds. Indeed the Arabic word al-Arab means "nomad".

Arabic is a Semitic language related to Accadian, Hebrew and Aramaic. It includes a number of dialects, particularly in the region of southern Arabia. Arabia may even have been the cradle of all the Semitic languages, in which case the expansion and diversification of these tongues would be the outcome of an early emigration following the progressive encroachment of the desert across the region in prehistoric times. This phenomenon, similar to the expansion of the Sahara several thousand years ago, forced the farmers to retreat to the rare cultivable zones, while the population of herdsmen and shepherds adapted to the changing environment at the price of a semi-nomadism imposed by the movement of the herds in search of grazing.

The Major Milestones

During Europe's glacial period, Arabia was thus more temperate and enjoyed a better rainfall than today. The discovery of flaked flint tools in large quantities demonstrates the presence of pre-historic peoples with a palaeolithic culture. But archaeological work is still too sparse to allow any firm conclusions about human evolution here in the early periods, especially as there has been no serious study of the deposit layers. There are also many tumuli, burial places sheltering small funeral chambers, which may date back to the neolithic or at least to the Bronze Age, 2000 years BC.

Whatever the truth of this, Arabia remained for a long time on the margins of historical development, isolated as it was by the desert from the great civilisations emerging just beyond its frontiers; a kind of insularity which is well reflected by the term used by Arabia's inhabitants for their country: "the isle of the Arabs".

The earliest references to these Arab peoples by their civilised neighbours date from a long way back. Around 2100 BC the Egyptians refer to these nomads from the East against whom they warred. But they also built up trading links with the producers of myrrh and incense—aromatics much sought after for embalming—and expeditions set out by sea for Southern Arabia and its fabulous riches.

It seems that in the 2nd millenium BC Arab navigators, taking advantage of the monsoon winds, already plied between the Middle East and India: from the Red Sea and the Persian Gulf to Ceylon, their sailing dhows carried on a seasonal trade in exotic products and, as merchants, they played an important role in the history of man's development. This is a point we shall have to return to a number of times to underline the historical function of this large-scale Arab commercial enterprise.

Towards the 9th century BC the Arabs appear again, this time in Assyro-Babylonian texts. A number of times the Assyrian troops had occasion to test their strength against tribes of Arab camel breeders and drivers. The princes of Saba even paid tribute to the rulers of Niniveh, And the Bible too refers to the Arab traders who brought aromatics to the Mediterranean port of Tyr.

The Persian king Cambyses, at the time of his conquest of Egypt, made an alliance with the Arabs to ensure water supplies for his troops. And finally, the Achaeminid empire included Arabia among its possessions, as is shown in the bas-reliefs of Persepolis. In 539 BC, the Persians organised a satrapy (a province with a governor), which they called Arabaya.

The South Arabian Civilization

Although it is still too soon to present a coherent picture of the early cultures which spread through Southern Arabia, where archaeological work has only begun and has so far only lifted one corner of the veil of mystery that lies over whole regions, we can nevertheless make some propositions that have been more or less certainly confirmed.

The first Arab kingdom mentioned in the Assyrian texts is that of Saba, referred to as a tributory of Sargon III and of Sennacherib, between 721 and 681 BC. The existence of this kingdom must go further back in time, for the First Book of Kings tells of a meeting between Solomon, who lived in the 10th century BC, and a Queen of Sheba, or Saba, who "came to Jerusalem with a very great train, with camels that bare spices, and very much gold, and precious stones".

This kingdom of Saba, however, did not reach the fullest extent of its power until the 6th, 5th and 4th centuries BC. Internally, it succeeded in unifying a number of principalities in southern Arabia, such as Ma'in and Qataban, and it seems to have been at the head of a confederation which also included Awsan, Himyar and the Hadramaut. Its influence reached as far as Ethiopia on the far side of the Red Sea: cities such as Axoum and Yeha, for example, bear the same architectural characteristics as the Sabaean capital of Marib.

Marib is enclosed in a rectangular perimeter wall 500 metres by 400 (550 yards by 440). The great temple, called the Awwam, stands within an oval temenos 125 metres (136 yards) in diameter and has rows of monolithic pillars nearly 8 metres (24 feet) high, remarkably finely dressed, which once supported cross-beams. The building methods show a Persian influence: walls of large stone blocks, squared and regular, consolidated by mortice joints, metal cramps and bond-stones.

The wealth of the region was based on the construction of three big dams for irrigation. The largest and most important was to collapse only in 575 AD after the fall of the Sabaean kingdom; today one can see the ruins of its walls, up to a height of 15 metres (50 feet), fine walls in which the cut stone blocks are 2 metres (6 ½ feet) long.

Among the still too rare finds of the kingdom of Saba to have been excavated so far, we should mention bronze statuary in which Greek techniques can be identified. This Greek influence can be seen, too, in the forms of the script in the Sabaean stone inscriptions. For the Sabaeans had their own script. This ancient South Arabian alphabet, with twenty-nine consonants and, in common with all Semitic alphabets, no vowels, derives from a "proto-Canano-Phœnician" script whose earliest examples come from Sinai and Palestine around 1700 BC.

Carefully engraved in alabaster, this Himyarite inscription dating from before Christ is in an alphabet of twenty-nine consonants and, like all Semitic scripts, without vowels (Sanaa Museum).

Remains of the ancient civilisation of the Himyars and foundations of buildings in fine, powerful cut stone are common in the Yemen but still await serious archaeological exploration.

This impressive bronze statue from Marib, cast by the lost wax method probably brought from Greece, represents a sovereign or Mukarrib of southern Arabia. Like Hercules he wears a lion skin, and the dagger in his belt is like those still used today by Yemeni tribesmen (Sanaa Museum).

The mark of Greece can be seen again in the minting of coins copied from Athenian tetradrachmas. And indeed the kingdom of Southern Arabia drew its wealth from a trade in aromatics with the Greek cities on one hand and the Achaemenid empire on the other. The close relations built up by the Arab traders abroad are born out by the discovery of inscriptions in Sabaean script outside Arabia, as far away as Egypt, Delos and Mesopotamia.

The high level of culture reached in the 6th and 5th centuries BC by the South Arabian kingdoms can be recognised not only through their monuments, fortifications and dam-building but equally through the political system by which the cities were governed. A kind of "parliamentary monarchy" seems to have existed, with assemblies of the tribes when there were important decisions to be taken.

In the 4th century BC state power in Southern Arabia was broken up with the rise of Ma'in and Qataban which both reached the height of their power in the 1st century before Christ.

The Nabataeans of Petra

The Sik, a formidable rock fault with walls 100 metres (300 feet) high, a kilometer (0.62 mile) long and so narrow in parts that two caravans could not pass, is the way into the Nabataean city of Petra. The entrance to the Sik was once marked by a triumphal arch.

Facing page:
At the exit to the Sik stands the fantastic facade, entirely cut out of the rock, of the Nabataean tomb called the Khazne Firaoun, or Treasury of Pharaoh, built in the 1st century BC. 32 metres (96 feet) high, it reproduces in carved rock the Hellenistic architectural orders.

While it was the mountains with their seasonal rains that earned the Arabian south its prosperity, in central Arabia the desert rules. Here one is far from that "happy Arabia", the Yemen (for indeed the Arabic word Yaman means happy), as much in contrast with the Arabia Deserta of the Hijaz as with the Arabia Petraea, stony Arabia, of the borders of Palestine. Land of rock and sand, these immense spaces, here and there merging into steppe, are the homeland of the Bedouin nomads. From one oasis to the next they drive their herds of goat and camels or lead their caravans.

The conditions imposed by these surroundings are hard. In spring, the camel-herders follow their beasts to those rare areas, at the foot of a hill or out in the desert expanses of the "empty quarter", where there is a brief flourish of greenery before the land returns to stony drought. Once summer has come, the search for grazing is more arduous, and brings the nomads along the dry beds of the "wadis" to the water sources controlled by sedentary farmers with whom they exchange livestock against cereals, vegetables and dates. Often the nomads went raiding to make up for their lack of food and the poverty of their wandering life with the shelter only of black goat-hair tents.

Originally, though, these nomads had neither camels (or, more accurately, dromedaries) nor horses—only the donkey as beast of burden to carry their tents, their few portable domestic articles and their provisions as the tribe moved on behind their herds. The camel seems to have been domesticated only between 2000 and 1000 BC, and the caravans first appeared in the 7th century BC. As for the horse, it came even later to southern Arabia; Xenophon in the 5th century BC describes Arabs on horseback hunting ostrich, not far from the Euphrates basin.

The First Intercontinental Trade

It remains a fact that trade alone was to allow these poor and inhospitable regions to escape their penury, thanks to the great caravans which brought the riches of the Yemen and the Hadramaut, their aromatic products, across the desert wastes, and which soon served also to transport exotic products coming from India and even China.

For this "incense route" across the Arabian peninsula from south to north, from the southern ports on the coast of the Indian Ocean to the Mediterranean trading centres of Gaza and Tyr, was to be transformed into a "spice route" and then a "silk route". The demand for products from the Orient increased unceasingly with the creation of the rich Greek cities in the 5th century BC, then with the vast territorial domi-

Strange marriage of natural cliff face and rock-cut architecture, the Khazne Firaoun of Petra counts among the most extraordinary creations of antiquity. It was the tomb of one of the Arab kings of Nabataea in the 1st century BC.

Detail of the circular tower crowning the facade of the Khazne of Petra: engaged columns with Ionic-Corinthian composite capitals and a frieze of vines are drawn entirely from the architectural language of Greece.

nions of the Hellenistic kingdoms born of Alexander's campaigns in Asia, and finally with the ascent of the Roman empire from the 1st century on.

As we have briefly mentioned above, the Arab navigators had very early learned to follow the southern coast from the peninsula round to India. It is probable that the first contacts were made through a purely coastal trade along the Omani coast, then from the south Persian coast and the mouth of the Indus to the Malabar coast and even Ceylon, where Indian ships relayed with the Arab dhows for the stage to Malacca, Indonesia and Indochina, visited in turn by Chinese junks. But the Arabs' coastal navigation must quite early have given way to the crossing of the Indian Ocean. Once launched on the high seas, the trading ships learned to make the best of the monsoon winds according to the season, to supply the Middle East with Far Eastern products. And so the trade in aromatics was complemented by the trade in goods in transit through Arabia. Around the beginning of our era, then, the Arabs acted—and in the highest secrecy, for the protection of their effective monopoly—as transporters of pearls, ivory, cinnamon, pepper, cloves, gold dust, ostrich feathers, cotton, silk and ceramics. In exchange they received and carried east gold and silver coin, wine, oil, wheat and such Greek and Roman craftsmens' work as vases, bronzes, goldwork, etc.

This traffic of caravans feeding international trade in fact followed two routes. Starting from a port not far from Bab al-Mandeb in Aden, in the state of Himyar, the route ran north across the country of Saba as far as the region of Najran, where it forked. One fork led north-west, passing not far from the place which later became Mecca, with a staging-post at Yathrib (Medina), then on to Hejira (al-Hijr) and then Petra, where it divided again to continue either to Gaza or to Tyr on the Mediterranean coast. The other fork across Arabia split off from the first near Najran to lead north-east, reaching the coast of the Persian Gulf opposite the island of Dilmun and rounding the gulf into Mesopotamia.

Very early on, the Arabs recognised the necessity of protecting the great arterial routes of their trade and to create staging-posts, generally fortified, along these axes; for the value of the caravans' cargoes, obviously, aroused the bitterest envy. Thus the Mineans in the 3rd century BC built fortresses along the route from southern Arabia, through the Hijaz and into Palestine. There the rudiments of civilisation developed. and the Nabataeans in the north of the peninsula were to benefit from this.

The Nabataeans came from north-west Arabia. The first mention of this Arab people dates from 647 BC when Assurbanipal, king of Assyria, numbers them among his enemies. But at that stage they did not yet occupy the site of Petra; they established themselves there a full century later. In the meantime Nabonidus, the last king of Babylon, had taken over the oasis of Tayma in south-east Nabataea and installed himself there, a few years after leaving the government of Babylon to the care of

At Petra the rock into which some of the tombs have been cut is veined in bright colours, a blaze of ochre and iron oxide reminiscent of wood grain.

Amid a fall of large rocks, the facades of the Nabataean tombs here combine classical pediments with a crenellated decoration with staggered merlons, as at Persepolis.

Beyond the oleander bushes scattered among the rocks of Petra, the Obelisk Tomb that marks the entrance to the Nabataean capital.

Bottom:
Cut into the living rock, the great theatre with its 34 tiers of seats could accommodate 3,000 spectators.

On the summit above Petra stands the small sacred obelisk, or baetyl, symbol of the Nabataeans' solar cult.

his son, in 550 BC. Tayma, on the caravan route between al-Hijr and the Euphrates, may have been the Nabataean capital before Petra.

The Rise of Petra

Petra, corresponding to the biblical Sela in the country of Edom, in the Arabia Petraea of the ancient geographers, had in fact been abandoned by the Edomites in the 6th century BC. Shortly afterwards the site was occupied by the Nabataeans, who made it the hub of their commercial world. Having been a province in the Persian empire since 539 BC, the region of northern Arabia had adopted Aramaic, the administrative language of the Achaeminids, for inscriptions, but Arabic was retained as the day to day language.

The rise of the Nabataeans of Petra took place between the 4th century BC and the 1st century AD. Antiochus III (218-217 BC) cites the Arabs of Petra at the time of his campaign against Egypt, and in 169 BC there is the first reference to a Nabataean ruler, Aretas, who is referred to as "tyrant of the Arabs" and so seems not to have taken the title of king, Aretas II however was "king of the Arabs". Between 120 and 96 BC he reigned over Syria, and his kingdom stretched as far as Egypt. His successor, Obodas I, inflicted a severe defeat on the Jewish king Alexander Janneus around 93 or 90 BC. At the beginning of his reign in 85 BC, Aretas III was called to Damascus where he was named King of Coelo-Syria; he minted bronze coins with a Greek text and called himself "Philhellene". His kingdom stretched southwards as far as the Hijaz. To ensure a solid base for himself on the caravan route to Damascus and

Antioch, he fortified Busra, a city which was to take on growing importance in the Roman period.

Petra was thus the capital of a kingdom in full expansion. The city itself overflowed with the riches coming from international trade: taxes, tolls and the profits of the busy trade in luxury goods for which the western world had an ever-growing appetite. Diodorus mentions that Alexander's lieutenant Antigone Monophtalmos (the one-eyed), who had wanted to bring Petra into subjection around 304 BC, had found in Petra, still a rocky labyrinthine den and yet to become the sumptuous city of Arab caravaneers, some 500 talents of silver—equivalent to 13 tons of precious metal, a talent weighing about 26 kilos (57 lbs). Three centuries later, then, one may imagine what must have been the wealth of this citadel, staging-post and warehouse of a vast domain at the junction of the two Hellenistic kingdoms of the Ptolemies and Seleucids.

The Discovery of the Site

For five or six centuries, Petra disappeared from the memory of mankind; from the crusades until the 19th century, even its name had vanished. It was the Swiss explorer Johann Ludwig Burckhardt, on his way between Damascus and Cairo, who heard his guide speak of a fabulous city in ruins. In 1812, he was the first European to penetrate, disguised as a Bedouin, into this labyrinth of rocks where the great stone monuments of the Nabataeans are carved out. But he dared not take even the least sketch, for fear of being unmasked. The first engravings of Petra to be published were the work of a Frenchman, Léon de Laborde, who visited the city in 1825, enticed by Burckhardt's account.

Visiting the ancient Nabatean capital today one can understand the stupefaction of these first travellers. In the heart of the Jordanian desert, between Red Sea and Dead Sea, in the wilderness of rock where a dry and torrid wind blows endlessly across a country with no sign of life, from the immensity of the djebels rises the city of Petra. To reach the city one must make one's way through a chaos of sheer rocks, through ravines hollowed out by the rare but tumultuous waters of the Wadi

Bottom:
Carved into pink, orange and purplish-red rock, the chambered tomb known as the Tomb of the Triclinium was designed for the celebration of a feast in which the whole family took part, with libations in honour of the deceased. The hall represents in stone a rich private house of the period.

Detail of the severe decoration of a doorway with pediment sculptured in rock. The capitals, rough-cut only, give a sober effect.

Musa, or River of Moses. Little by little one penetrates a gorge overhung by high sheer cliffs. This dark defile is the Sik, once entered through a Roman-style triumphal arch which was only to be carried away in 1896 by one of the wadi's catastrophic floods. Here passed thousands of caravans loaded with riches from the Yemen, India or China.

Guarded by this gorge, so narrow that two horses cannot pass each other, Petra the mysterious could grow rich without fear of raiders. For this formidable entrance, this corridor cut in the red sandstone, 100 metres (300 feet) deep and a kilometre (0.6 mile) long, constitutes an extraordinary defense for the site. At the end of this colossal gully, the travellers's wonderstruck gaze meets the unexpected and awe-inspiring sight of a magnificent monument, emerging at the last moment from behind a narrow crack: the Khazne Firaoun, or Pharaoh's Treasury as the Bedouin have christened it, forgetful of their own glorious past.

Entirely cut from the rock of the Sik's vertical cliff face, the Khazne is a funerary monument whose facade, in Hellenistic style, is of colossal proportions: 32 metres (100 feet) high, equivalent to ten floors of a modern building! It is a marvel of architecture in rock, with two ranges of columns, the lower a colonnaded portico completely detached from the body of the rock. This gives access to the hall which once contained the tomb of a Nabataean ruler. The upper range of columns supports a broken pediment framing a kind of cylindrical central tower with engaged columns. The Khazne must also have born large sculptures representing the Nabataean gods, but these have since been destroyed.

The Khazne thus serves as a sumptuous prelude on the way in to the city of Petra. Further on, the rocky gorge marked out at intervals by rock-carved tombs narrows one last time before opening out onto the capital. The great bowl where once the city stood is circled by mountains whose cliffs shelter hundred of underground chambers cut into the rock. From all sides their tall facades, imitating the architecture of the town's secular buildings (though none of these remain), appear against the rock walls. Like a city of troglodytes, Petra shows no more than these tombs with doorways yawning onto silence and abandon.

And in its theatre with tiers of seats cut into the rock, which could hold 3,000 people, twenty centuries ago there resounded the works of the Greek tragedians before the dazzled merchants of this gateway to the desert. For wealth had brought with it luxury and the arts, and here, right on the edge of Arabia, Aeschylus and Sophocles proclaimed the destiny of man before cultured Bedouins who could understand the Greek of the Hellenistic "koïne".

The surprising architecture of Petra weds the raw cliffs to the proud Corinthian facades, and so constitutes one of the most fascinating conjunctions between art and nature. The clarity of design of a pediment here sometimes takes on the perfect rigour of a blue-print. And the hands of sculptors—engaged at great cost and brought from Syria or Asia Minor by the rich Nabataean merchants—have disciplined the wildness of the site, at the same time not hesitating to give their full value to the variegated patterns of the rock. For here, iron oxides have given to the sandstone all shades of colour from mauve to orange, through browns, russet reds, fawns and ochres, with veins of white, blue or grey... Faced with this flamboyant display, what must have been the stupefaction of Laborde and his companions discovering at each step a new monument, each one more luxurious than the last, and which they christened the Three-Storey Tomb, the Corinthian Tomb, the Latin Tomb or the Tomb of the Urn.

The world of the dead rules everywhere in the narrow valleys that radiate from the city. Every rock is marked with the seal of funerary monuments. The Tomb of the Roman Soldier, for example: its three niches hold the statues of men dead and buried two thousand years ago, though weather damage has reduced to nothing the faces of these glorious provincial governors.

But if the dead haunt Petra, the living had nonetheless taken posses-

Bottom:
The Tomb of the Roman Soldier, so named by the first discoverers of the site on bringing to light a latin inscription. The three niches contain effigies of three legionnaires buried here two thousand years ago.

Hollowed out of the small valleys around Petra, cisterns collected the run-off water from the mountains to supply the city's inhabitants and the few cultivated fields.

sion of every scrap of cultivable earth to plant cheerful orchards on them. And scattered in every small valley are tanks to collect water from the rare winter rains, for a highly developed irrigation system had turned Petra into a veritable oasis in the midst of a dry and sun-baked universe. And the Nabataeans, by means of a vast network of aqueducts, drained the least trickle of water from the Umm al-Biyara massif, literally the "mother of reservoirs", which overlooks the town and reaches an altitude of 1160 metres (3800 feet).

Al Dayr, Swan-song of the Nabataeans

On the heights of Petra, the Dayr is perhaps the most fantastic of the Nabataean monuments: even more audacious than el-Khazne, this tomb with its rock facade 50 metres (150 feet) wide and nearly 45 metres (135 feet) high looks onto a panorama sweeping across Sinai and as far as the Dead Sea. The elaborate style of this architectural sculpture with its powerful recesses and projections, the vigorous modelling of its outlines, its clean-cut capitals, all make the Dayr the true swan-song of Petra.

For in the 2nd century AD, after the victory of the Syrian legate Cornelius Palma who occupied Petra with his troops in 106 under Trajan's reign, the country became part of the Roman empire under the name of the "province of Arabia", with Busra as capital.

Palmyra, Pearl of the Desert

Detail of the triumphal arch at Palmyra, built around 200 AD. Arch and pillars bear a richly sculptured decoration.

Tadmor, or Palmyra, at the heart of a wilderness of burning sand, offered the gentle cool of its palm groves swept by the great desert winds to the caravans which made it their staging-post. It was an obligatory port of call for merchants coming from Mesopotamia and the Persian Gulf, up the Euphrates and across to the Phœnician ports on the Mediterranean. And it was, so it is said, founded by Solomon... But this verdant resting place in the midst of a furnace of sand and salt only enters history after its conquest by Alexander the Great. Greek colonists arriving to join the Arabs and Aramaeans who lived here made it a flourishing city where Greek and the Semitic dialects soon mingled.

Two kinds of wealth attracted man to the heart of the wilderness: life-giving water, and gold. At this cross-roads between the western world and the Orient, prosperous merchants exchanged silks from China, precious stones from the Buddhist kingdoms of northern India and Indonesian spices against gold, the purple dye of Tyr, pottery, glass and Syrian wines. For Palmyra remained for several centuries the hub of all the trade passing between Asia and the Mediterranean.

The Roman conquest at first facilitated the rise of the city by diverting onto a new route a large proportion of the traffic which had until then gone through the Arabian peninsula: ships now came right up the Persian Gulf to transfer their cargoes onto river boats which brought them up the Euphrates; the Arab carriers turned to caravans for transport only between Circesium, halfway up the Euphrates, and Tyr or Sidon, or indeed Antioch—with a necessary stop-off at Palmyra. But if Rome made possible the city's wealth, it was also Rome that caused its loss.

Splendour in an Oasis

Discovered at the end of the 17th century by English travellers, the ruins of the caravan city still astonish visitors to Palmyra: colonnades stretching as far as the eye can see: temples, porticos and triumphal arches stand between the dunes, witness to the glory that once surrounded this capital of an immense but ephemeral empire.

Buildings of great luxury, whose imposing ruins still stand today amid the sands, were commissioned from Greek and Roman architects and planners by the chiefs of rich Arab tribes wanting to give their city all the pomp of an imperial capital—just as today the emirs of the Gulf call on American or Japanese engineers and builders to erect the metropoles of their oil kingdoms. For in the 3rd century, all the spices and exotic products destined for Rome passed by this oasis, and the Romans had to pay exorbitant taxes on oriental goods. The emperors were even obliged to forbid men to wear silk togas, to keep the treasury from running dry. All the gold of Rome flowed into the coffers of the "shipping agents" of international trade in Palmyra. The Palmyran Arabs were even to refuse devalued "aurei" after the great financial crash of 259-260 when the emperor Valerian was taken prisoner by the Persians.

The ruins we can see today in the Syrian desert show that Palmyra was, in a way, the Wall Street or Stock Exchange of Antiquity. The great avenues seethed with a motley of peoples—Greek and Levantine merchants, Arab caravaneers, Bedouin warriors, Phœnician money-changers, courtesans and matrons passed by in the shade of the porticos. Black slaves and Persian traders, priests of Baal or of Isis, Jews and Christians crowded these ostentatious streets.

In the sacred enclosure of the great Temple of Bel, inside the sanctuary dedicated to the Sun god, fluted columns still stand which must once have been surmounted by Corinthian capitals, though the gilded bronze corbels have now disappeared. At the centre of the immense temenos, which covered 5 hectares (12 acres), the cella enclosing the golden statue of the god was open only to the priests of the divine triad of Palmyra.

Funerary stele representing a noblewoman of Palmyra. The wide, expressive eyes, the fine face, a hair-band and a full draped robe : this 3rd century Palmyran beauty has retained all her grace and nobility.

A portico of the great avenue at Palmyra, seen through an arch of one of the lateral arcades. Brackets two-thirds of the way up the Corinthian columns once supported statues of the magistrates and benefactors of this city of the sands.

Overleaf (pp. 24-25):
The great colonnade of Palmyra's principal street, several hundred yards long, stands out in the Syrian desert. The columns have been eroded at their base by sand-storms. Looking at these awe-inspiring ruins one can imagine the luxury and splendour of the city where the wealth of East and West converged.

23

Bottom right:

The small temple of Baal-Shamin, built between 67 and 130 AD, is consecrated to the great cosmic god, the "Lord of the Heavens", who together with the gods of sun and moon made up the heavenly triad of Palmyra. On a rocky spur overlooking the site one can see a medieval Arab fortress.

This young Palmyran, perhaps a merchant, seems lost in melancholy reverie. Greek sculpture here comes together with Persian art, especially in the treatment of the hair and beard. This funerary stele bears an Aramaic inscription.

The towers of the necropolis of Palmyra, outside the city in the desert. In this Valley of Tombs, one may note in particular the Tower of Iamblicus (right), a five-storey building dating from 83 AD.

An Ephemeral Empire

At the beginning of the 3rd century it was Odaynath, the chief of an Arab tribe, who ruled the city. His descendent Odaynath II ruled from 258 to 266 and won the confidence of Rome through his victorious campaign against the Persians of the Sassanid dynasty whose capital was at Ctesiphon on the Tigris. Profiting from the chaos in the Roman empire, where Postumus had usurped power in Gaul and Persians, Goths, Franks and Alamanni had invaded simultaneously, a debacle culminating in the capture of Valerian by the Persians in 260, Palmyra carried its troops and its gods right across the East of the ancient world. Odaynath defeated Shapur and proclaimed himself king of Mesopotamia. The archers of Palmyra conquered the Nile valley and Anatolia.

And when Queen Zenobia came to the throne of this proud city of the sands, she was able to proclaim herself Empress of the Orient. The wide spread of the worship of Bel and the gold of the caravans enabled her to rule over Syria, Palestine, Mesopotamia, Egypt and Asia Minor together. And from the stronghold of this isolated oasis in the Syrian desert arose a deadly menace to Rome. Confrontation was inevitable, and the emperor Aurelian took it on himself to take up the challenge of this Empress of the Orient who thought herself invincible in the heart of these protective wastes. The accumulated wealth and the proud squadrons of fast dromedaries which had established Palmyra's supremacy over the desert and the rich lands of the Fertile Crescent could not save the city. Destiny was on the march with the legions of Rome.

Aurelian, whose principate began in 270, determined to redress the threatened situation he had inherited with the empire, though Claudius had already partially restored the situation by defeating the Goths the previous year. Aurelian set out to organise a campaign against Palmyra. In 272 the Romans besieged the city, having already routed the Palmyran troops at Antioch and at Emesus. Zenobia managed to flee the city to go to seek help from the Persians, but was captured before she could cross the Euphrates; she was paraded as a spectacle in Rome for the emperor's triumph, and died a captive there.

Palmyra capitulated. But hardly had Aurelian left Syria when the town rose in revolt against the Roman garrison and massacred it. Aurelian returned, and this time let his troops pillage and burn the rich city, had the walls pulled down and humbled forever the pearl of the desert. When the legions had gone, nothing remained of Palmyra but

the tombs around a scattered village. It was never to rise again; its power was extinguished like Petra's before it.

It was the ruins of the tall funerary towers where rich Palmyrans were buried that most struck the first visitors. Keeping vigil over the desert at the gates of the dead city, they seem to proclaim the vanity of all glory and all wealth. Under the brilliant and immutable Syrian sky the wind whistles through their gaping doorways.

The great of Palmyra had dared to rise against Rome. Magistrates who managed the world as if it were no more than a prosperous business, strategists whose nomad warriors had ruled by fear, where are they now? Their sumptuous tombs with painted ceilings, their funerary niches, all are plundered. All that remains are the high pilasters with their acanthus capitals and the sculptured effigies of the illustrious dead.

But it is precisely these high-relief sculptures showing forgotten personalities that haunt this wilderness; their eyes search the shadows, the carving restores to us the moving, expressive faces of the noblemen of Palmyra. They give a human face to the extraordinary adventure of these Arab merchants who were able to bring together the far ends of the earth to circulate material pleasures. And they bring back to us how sweet life must have been in Palmyra, queen of the sands.

The sanctuary of the great Temple of Bel at Palmyra, standing on an esplanade surrounded by a portico 225 metres (205 yards) square, was consecrated in 32 AD. The tall columns once bore bronze capitals. Inside the naos, the adyton contained the divine triad.

27

Hatra the Free City

A stele from Hatra representing the sun god Helios-Shamash, dating from the 2nd century AD.

The Romans' confrontation with the Parthians, then with the Sassanids who succeeded them in 227 AD, was one of the fiercest and deadliest of the whole age of Antiquity. It dragged on for six hundred years. Its dates alone are eloquent: in 34-37 AD, a Roman intervention in Parthia; in 58-63, Corbulo Domitius' campaign; in 114-117 Trajan forces his way into Parthia; in 162-166 Verus and Avidius Cassius at war with the Parthians; in 195, campaigns against the Parthians under Septimus Severus; in 197-199 the annexation of Mesopotamia; in 231, the first war against the Sassanids; in 241-244, the second Persian war; in 260, Valerian falls prisoner to Shapur; in 281, the Persian campaign of the emperor Carus; further Persian wars in 297, 338 and 363, then a treaty between Persians and Romans in 381. War breaks out again around 418 against Bahram V and ends in the Hundred Years Peace of 422; the Byzantines ally with the Persians against the Huns, but the treaty is broken in 497 and war again breaks out in 502 under Anasthasius, then in 527 under Justinian; the campaign of 540 ends in a truce in 555; but Justin II takes up battle again in 572, defeats the Persians and signs a new truce in 575. In the 7th century, shortly before the rise of Arab power after the preaching of Mohammed, the pitiless struggle between Byzantium and the Sassanids made the victories of Islam easier.

The Arabs have always been pushed by the necessities of their harsh country to try and escape their nomadic condition and establish themselves in more hospitable regions. So it was that they were drawn, as we have seen, by Palestine and Syria, and also by the rich Mesopotamian basin. At first their expeditions were limited to raids. Then they ventured to establish staging posts for their caravans in that region of shifting frontiers between the two great powers of the day.

Gateway and Sanctuary of the Desert

On the borders of the Parthian empire, the city of Hatra is one of the most brilliant examples of this policy of infiltration marking the first great Arab expansion, before the Hegira. Hatra has only been scientifically excavated since 1951, and our knowledge of the city is still quite limited. For a long time it was considered a purely Parthian town. But as at Petra and Palmyra, a better evaluation of available facts now allows us to number it among the works of the Arabs.

The visitor finds himself astonished as he arrives across the Iraqui desert to the ancient fortified city of Hatra, between the Tigris and Euphrates and halfway between Assur and Dura Europos: he discovers monuments evocative of the world of Greece and Rome with its Ionic columns and its pediments, but with vaulted iwans which tie it also to

Whole and detail of the Hatra sanctuary with its double Ionic and Corinthian peristyle, recently brought to light by Iraqi archaeologists.

29

Bas-relief of the eagle god of the Arabs, Hadad, over an aramaic inscription; from Hatra, and dating from the 2nd century AD (Mossul Museum).

A very lovely statue from Hatra, representing Sanatruq II, "king of the Arabs": 2 metres (6 feet) high, and recently unearthed, it dates from 220 to 240 AD. The highly original style is like a prediction of Western medieval sculpture. The king wears a tall crown in the Parthian style, and richly decorated robes (Bagdad Museum).

Parthian architecture, although these iwans are built of dressed stone and so are more reminiscent of Roman work than of the Parthians' brick archways. The town of Hatra was built on a circular plan 6 kilometres (3.7 miles) in circumference, fortified by three concentric walls separated by dry moats, and with guard towers and bastions. There is a gate at each of the cardinal points. In the centre, a square temenos contains temples which must have held an important place in the royal cult. The circular city walls relate the town-planning of Hatra to a Persian tradition which possibly goes right back to the Assyrians' military camps, and which is also to be found at Gur (Firuzabad) and Ctesiphon and later, in the Islamic age, in the "round city" of Bagdad built by the Abbassid al-Mansur.

From the time of its foundation, the city held resources which assured its independence, besides the international trade which made up its

Head of a king or god, from Hatra: it could almost have come straight from a European Gothic doorway (Mossul Museum).

Above left:
Detail of Sanatruq II, with beard and moustache. His expression is intense, his gaze proud (Bagdad Museum).

wealth: having diverted the course of a seasonal river, the inhabitants were able to create huge reservoirs from which they could irrigate the arid plain and transform it into a veritable garden, with palm groves and fields of wheat. Each house, in addition, had its own well.

It was in the first century AD that the Arab tribes founded the city, which takes its name from "al-Hadr" in Arabic, equivalent to the latin term "castrum" for a permanent fortified camp. Among the inscriptions discovered at Hatra one can find names of Iranian, Aramaic and Arabic origin. The first ruler of the city was called Nasr; the kings who followed him took names that were common among the Arsacids: Vologese and Sanatruq I and II. Their sons, however, bore Arab names.

Hatra victoriously resisted sieges by Trajan in 117 and again in 198 and 199 by Septimus Severus, who never succeeded in seizing the town even though he had annexed Mesopotamia. In fact the city held a formidable weapon against its assailants: the "fire of Hatra" hurled by war machines and composed of bitumen, naphtha and sulphur—the oil-rich nature of the land already being a factor of its independence!

The eclectic culture of Hatra is expressed in inscriptions written in oriental Aramaic, but in a very particular script. The Hatrian alphabet was to influence Dura Europus in particular. But it is according to

The Arab eagle god Hadad, symbol of the city of Hatra, appears in several places within the sanctuaries.

Top:
Triad of Hatrian divinities in alabaster: the crowned goddesses carry palms and a mirror. Traces of polychrome can still be seen (Mossul Museum).

Facing page, top right:
A goddess from Hatra, probably Ishtar-Atargatis (the Roman Venus), found during recent excavations. This richly polychromed alabaster sculpture with inlaid eyes is a good example of the art of Hatra in the 3rd century (Mossul Museum).

Facing page, bottom:
Stele consecrated to the Hatran god of the underworld, who carries an axe and cthonian serpents (Mossul Museum),

the Seleucid calendar that the documents are dated, with the year 1 at 312 BC.

The main sovereigns who governed this "free city" were of the 2nd and 3rd centuries AD. Vologese of Hatra, Sanatruq I and Sanatruq II were all entitled "King of the Arabs", so it seems that the city had succeeded in extending its influence over the tribes to the south of the Euphrates.

Its religion mingled eastern gods with Greek, with many an eloquent parallel: the great goddess Allât became Athena, Hercules corresponds to Malek, Hades to Nergal, Helios to Shamash. The Syrian god Baal Shamin of Palmyra is there too. And the cult of the Sun occupied the predominant place; it was to the Sun god that the defeat of Septimus Severus was attributed. And finally the eagle, the Arab god Hadad, was the city's symbol.

After three centuries of existence, often opulent, as an independent city, Hatra was to collapse not under assault by the Romans but in the face of the Sassanid Shapur I, in 241, the same Shapur who was to take the emperor Valerian prisoner in 260. As Palmyra was put to plunder by the legions of Aurelian, so Hatra was sacked by the Persians. Soon it was to disappear from the memory of mankind. But it had shone with a lively brilliance in the firmament of History. For three full centuries, this staging-post for Arab caravans carrying the riches of the Far East as far as Antioch had drawn its profits from the traffic of cargo between Persia and Rome.

The Arab World Asserts Itself

A first Arab expansion had thus led the tribal chiefs to implant themselves in that no-man's-land of the desert between Syria and the Euphrates. Apart from Petra, Palmyra and Hatra, cities such as Emesus and Edessa were part of their sphere of influence. There were even Arabs who rose to the very highest posts of the Roman Empire. The wife of Septimus Severus and mother of Caracalla was an Arab from Emesus, Julia Domna. Her sister Julia Maesa was to succeed in putting two of her own grandsons on the throne as emperors: Elagabel who reigned from 218 to 222 and Alexander Severus, from 222 to 235. These were Arabs, members of a dynasty of high priests of Emesus, where the famous Black Stone was worshipped, a symbol of the Sun; they even tried to impose its cult in Rome. Finally there is Philip the Arab who, thanks to his cavalry of Bedouin nomads, had succeeded in seizing the throne by a bold stroke and reigned from 244 to 249. He it was who organised a new expedition in Persia, whose failure was a bitter blow—as witness the Sassanid bas-reliefs at Nakh-e-Rustam where he surrendered to Shapur. The philosopher Plotinus, who had gone with him hoping to reach India by way of Persia, only just escaped.

But the Arab contribution to Roman civilisation was not restricted to providing masters of the Empire. The philosopher Porphyrus was an Arab; so were Longinus, Iamblicus and Heliodorus. In addition, the great religious centres of Palmyra, Hatra and Emesus constitute, in a way, places of worship which foreshadow the role Mecca was later to play: pilgrimages were organised for the faithful, and the worship of meteoric rocks or baetyls (from the Arabic "Beit-El" or House of God) was widespread there.

Lakhmids and Ghassanids: the Christian Arabs

The power of the two great antagonists, Rome and the Sassanids, had put an end to the Arab implantation in the great cities of the Parthian and Hellenistic-Roman type. But from the 5th century on, new Arab emirates established themselves in the desert zones and on the desert's edge. Thus the Lakhmid kings of Hira, on the Euphrates, near Ctesiphon, claimed to be masters of all the Arabs and ruled over the

Bas-relief from Hatra showing the god of the underworld, Hades/Nergal, dressed in the Parthian style with horseman's tunic and trousers. The god is carrying a sword at his side and a double-bladed axe in his right hand. To one side of him are serpents and a crab (Cancer), symbols of the underworld, and a small figure of his wife (Proserpine); on the other side, a religious emblem related to the Roman legions' standards. The god, horned and bearded, is crowned by a small effigy of an eagle with spread wings (Mossul Museum).

Syro-Iraqui desert. Originally pagan, the Lakhmids were converted to Nestorian Christianity. The Byzantines set up their "cousins" the Ghassanids in opposition to them—and they too, around 500 AD, became Christian, but of the Syrian monophysite sect.

These states of Ghassan and Hira created a close blend of the Aramaic and Graeco-Roman cultures. The Ghassanid king Harith (or Aretas) ibn Jabala's victory in 529 over the other Arab tribes earned him political recognition from Justinian, who conceded to him control over the territories of the Yarmuk basin. In the principality of Hira, the Lakhmid dynasty also formed a "buffer state". But this was swept away in 604 by new Arab tribes which defeated the Persians and established themselves in the region.

One of the reasons for the sudden new importance of central Arabia, and the Hijaz in particular, on the eve of the Hegira, was the generalised disorder following the incessant wars of the 6th century between Byzantium and Persia. This insecurity forced the merchants to abandon the caravan route between the Persian Gulf and the Mediterranean through Mesopotamia and the Syrian desert. From then on, the route through the Yemen and Arabia was re-established. And it was Mecca which became the central staging-post of trade and transit. An oligarchy of rich importers, under the impulse of the Quraysh tribe, established there a kind of republic of merchants. At its head, an assembly of powerful businessmen, called the Mala, was made up of elected notables who organised the city's political economy.

Mohammed, Prophet of Islam

The archangel Gabriel gives Mohammed, on his knees and surrounded by a golden halo, his mission: to carry the word of God. On the left is Fatima. Miniature from the manuscript "The Life of Mohammed" (Top Kapi Museum, Istambul).

Facing page:
Mohammed enthroned in heaven, before the angels and the archangel Gabriel. This is the ascension, the "night journey" when the Prophet beheld the face of God. ("Life of Mohammed", Top Kapi Museum, Istambul).

Mohammed is one of the great founders of monotheistic religions to have emerged in the Middle East, following on from Moses and Jesus Christ. He explicitly took up the tradition of the Pentateuch and recognised a close relationship between the three great religions founded on the Bible; Judaism, Christianity and Islam. He called the believers of all three religions "the people of the Book".

The Prophet's influence has made its mark right across the world. Today some 500 million Moslems live according to the precepts contained in the Koran (literally the "recitation"), the compilation of all the revelations received by Mohammed, whose text in Arabic includes 114 chapters or surahs.

Mohammed was born around 570 AD in Mecca, son of a once rich but ruined family. He was orphaned at an early age, losing his mother when he was two and his father when he was eight. Brought up by his uncle, he led caravans from Mecca into Syria, where he got to know the Christian community. At the age of twenty-five he married a rich widow fifteen years his senior; they had several children, though the only child to survive was Fatima, his daughter, who was to marry Mohammed's first cousin Ali.

Mohammed's Mission

God's call to Mohammed came through the intermediary of the Archangel Gabriel. Mohammed was then forty, and set to work preaching in Mecca; but his preaching was generally met with scepticism by the city's rich merchants. They did not believe in the mission of this man who set himself in the direct line of biblical prophets and spoke of Abraham and Ishmael, Adam, Noah, Moses, Lot, Joseph, Elijah and Elisha, as well as of John the Baptist, Jesus and Mary.

We should remember, in this context, that Christianity had come into Arabia in the 3rd century. The oasis of Najran, a Christian centre which had its own bishop, was the bastion of the new faith, and in the 5th century adopted Nestorianism. But it was above all the Jewish religion that had developed in Arabia before the coming of Islam. We know that one Himyarite sovereign was converted to Judaism in 523, along with many of his subjects. The Christians, victims of much persecution, were burnt in their thousands, and this was the pretext for an Abyssinian military intervention which put an end to the Himyarite dynasty. The Abyssinian Negus ruled in Southern Arabia right up to 570, even attempting an expedition against Mecca with a troop of elephants.

But to return to the story of Mohammed: faced with threats from the rich merchants who saw with some anxiety that he was making converts,

عاد قومن هلاك قلدومرسنك دوشمنلروكى داخى شويله هلاء
قلايم ددى اندن رسول عليه السلام اول برسنى دخى ايكرو

اوقدى ايتدى سنيه مؤكلسن ددى اول فرشته دخى اينك
بن دكرزلوصولراوستنه موكلم حق تعالى بلوندن انت يغمورلرى

35

the Prophet went into exile. Together with his faithful he emigrated to the oasis of Yathrib, which became thenceforth Medina al-Nebi, the City of the Prophet, or Medina. The date of this "exodus", which took place in 622, marks the beginning of the Islamic calendar—the Hegira. Mohammed took the leadership of this oasis community and there he pursued his mission for ten years. He expressed his revelations in a language of admirable power and lyricism, bringing Arabic to its most classic purity.

A shrewd politician and an able diplomat, chief of a community whose interests he did not neglect, Mohammed even succeeded in cutting the caravan trail to Mecca, for he wanted to re-enter that city in triumph. But he did not neglect his religious work, and in his own house, the house of a chief of Medina's community, he founded the first Moslem place of communal prayer, the first mosque. At first it was towards Jerusalem that the faithful were to face for their prayers, this to demonstrate Mohammed's view of Islam as a faith in continuity with the Jewish and Christian religions, for which the Holy City is symbolic both of Solomon's Temple (by that time destroyed) and of the Holy Sepulchre. For the creation of his mosque, bordered by porticos of

Detail of a miniature from "The Life of Mohammed" showing the Ka'ba, or Black Stone of Mecca.

Mohammed, on horseback, confronting the Byzantine troops. The Prophet preaches the Jihad, the holy war which earned Islam its astonishing expansion (Miniature from "The Life of Mohammed", Top Kapi Museum, Istambul).

palm trunks supporting a palm roof, he drew inspiration from a formula going back to pre-Islamic sanctuaries such as that at Huqqa (from the 2nd century BC), which also has a courtyard at the centre. This mosque in the Prophet's house, built on a square plan about 50 metres (160 feet) square, was bounded by a mud wall. This wall, on the north side, facing the faithful as they turned towards Jerusalem to pray, formed the first "qibla".

The Triumph at Mecca

In 624 there was a definitive rupture with Judaism: the Jews denied the authenticity of the Prophet as God's messenger. This put into question the orientation towards Jerusalem. The new orientation of prayer, towards Mecca, was promulgated in the wake of certain dramatic developments. In the sixth year of the Hegira, Mohammed wished to

Facing page:
At the centre of the sanctuary at Mecca, the Ka'ba, or Black Stone, around which pilgrims perform the rite of circumambulation. This is the primary centre of the Moslem world, on which is focussed the faith of 500 million believers.

Fragment of a page of an antique Koran in Kufic script, from the 8th or 9th century.

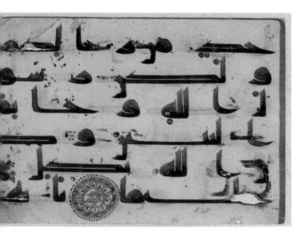

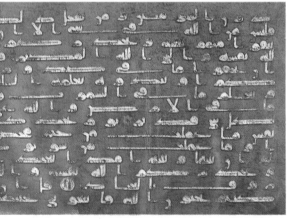

Page of a fine Koran in Kufic script from the 9th century: the white text on a deep blue ground gives a superbly luminous effect.

put an end to the state of warring antagonism with the Meccans, and set out on a pilgrimage to his city of origin. But the troops of Mecca blocked his way, and he and his followers were unable to enter the city. An agreement was finally signed stipulating that the Moslems could carry out their pilgrimage in peace the following year during a truce. This was in 629. A year later, having gathered a strong assembly of troops, Mohammed marched on Mecca, entered in triumph and established his military occupation. He entered the Ka'ba, the temple of the Black Stone (baetyl) which was the old place of pilgrimage of the current religion, and smashed the idols in the sanctuary—but he preserved the cult of the Black Stone itself, considering it to have been founded by Abraham and his son Ishmael, common ancestors of the Jews and Arabs. From then on it was towards the Ka'ba that all Islamic mosques were to be turned, beginning with the house of the Prophet. This time its southern wall was given a portico as the north side had been. This transformation, easily done since the city of Medina lies more or less in a direct line between Jerusalem and Mecca, made the Moslems' first place of prayer into the "mosque with two qiblas". Thus from 630 AD, Mecca becomes the focus of Islam, and there Mohammed established the pilgrimage every good Moslem hopes to make at least once in his life.

At this juncture Mohammed returned to Medina, where he died in 632 after putting an end to his preaching work. His religion brought, with the Koran, a complete divine and human law, including equally prescriptions for the ritual of prayer and juridical, social, cosmological and eschatological laws. Through this Mohammed left his people the certainties which were to dynamise the Arab tribes under the flag of the "holy war", the jihad, conceived of as a collective obligation of the Moslem community. Thenceforth the knights of the faith swept across the world of Antiquity.

The Age of Conquests

At the time of the Arab expansion, the struggle between Byzantines and Sassanids was growing more acute: the 626, Heraclius ruled an empire from which Syria, Palestine and Asia Minor had already been torn. The Persians laid siege to Constantinople. Heraclius redressed the situation by attacking the enemy on all fronts; he took Ctesiphon and drove the Persian troops out of the whole empire. The territorial power of Byzantium was restored, but the two antagonists were both exhausted.

On the death of Mohammed, internal struggles broke out among the Arabs. Abu-Bakr, one of the Prophet's fathers-in-law, became caliph, or head of the Moslem community. Then Omar, his successor, resolved the antagonisms by beginning the explosive expansion of Islam.

He conquered Palestine and Syria, crushed Heraclius in the Yarmuk valley in 636. Jerusalem and Damascus fell in 638. On the eastern front the Arab horsemen crossed the Euphrates as early as 635, sacking Ctesiphon, the Sassanid capital, in 637. And in 642 their victory in the battle of Nihawand opened up to them the plains of Iran.

Towards the west, Egypt was conquered in 640 and Tripolitania was taken in 642; from here, raids were launched westwards into Berber territory. To the east, the conquerors reinforced their power over Persia by taking Afghanistan in 655.

In this first Arab empire, Medina acted as a capital for the caliphs. In 644, it was Uthman who led the destiny of the Islamic world. On his assassination in 656, the territories held by the Arabs were equal to the greatest Empires of Antiquity, reaching from Tunisia to the gates of India. And this formidable expansion continued under the rule of the Umayyads of Damascus.

Interior view of the Dome of the Rock, Jerusalem: the two concentric ambulatories are designed for the ritual of circumambulation around the stone on which Abraham sacrificed a lamb instead of his son Isaac, and from which Mohammed rose to heaven on his Night Journey. Antique columns with Corinthian capitals, mosaics on a gold ground, polychrome marbles and arches with voussoirs in alternating colours, all derive from Byzantine art. This holy place of the Islamic faith was erected in 687 by architects commissioned by the caliph Abd al-Malik.

The Glory of the Umayyads

Detail of the luxuriant decoration of the Dome of the Rock: gilded Corinthian capitals on marble or porphyry columns, black and white archstones, mosaics of vines on a gold background.

Top:
The Dome of the Rock, Jerusalem: the central rotunda with its dome over the sacred rock. Two columns to one pillar alternate in a regular rhythm around the rock.

After the assassination of the caliph Uthman, the Prophet's cousin and son-in-law Ali succeeded him at the head of the empire. But trouble broke out between the Arab tribes and seriously threatened the unity of the Arab world. In 660, the seizure of power by Mu'awiyah in Damascus, where he had been governor of the city for twenty years, marked the foundation of the Umayyad dynasty. With the authority of Ali already in question, Mu'awiyah, chief of a noble family from Mecca, was able to impose his own will. His first act of government was to transfer the centre of empire from Medina to Damascus, at one stroke escaping the internal intrigues of the rich and powerful lords of Arabia and establishing a capital closer to the geographical centre of the empire, from where he could better survey the theatres of war. And in Damascus he had all the personnel of the Byzantine administrative structures who had stayed on after the conquest, and whose influence was increasing all the time.

These upheavals mark a brief pause in the triumphant expansion of the Arab armies. But once Mu'awiyah had consolidated his position as caliph, after the assassination of Ali in 661 and with the Islamisation of the new territories under way, the forward march began anew. In 670, Moslem troops crossed the Oxus (Amu-Darya) and broke into central Asia. Having conquered Anatolia, the Arabs laid siege to Constantinople in 673; but they were unable to seize the town and withdrew in 678, recognising that Byzantine mastery of the seas meant that the Moslems could defeat them only if they too possessed a powerful fleet of warships in the Mediterranean.

From 680 to 683, Yazid I was caliph at Damascus, his reign beginning with the assassination of Ali's son Hussein. The deaths of the Prophet's direct descendants created a new schism within Islam: the minority of Shiites (as the partisans of Ali called themselves), in opposition to the Sunnite orthodoxy, founded the doctrine of the Imams, according to which only Mohammed's own bloodline could be considered keepers of religious knowledge and could direct the Moslem community. From this schism, shattering the unity of the Moslem world only some sixty years after the death of the Prophet, flowed the incessant struggles and bloody wars which were to earn the Shiites a long list of martyrs and taint the Islamic world with the blood of innumerable victims.

When Yazid I, considered responsible for the murder of Hussein, acceded to power, a violent reaction set in in Arabia: Ibn al-Zubayr, a cousin of Mohammed, refused to recognise the Umayyads' authority and pronounced himself caliph in Mecca. He ruled as anti-caliph over the Moslems of Arabia for ten years. Medina expelled the Umayyads' representatives from the holy city. Troops from Damascus, under the caliphate of Abd al-Malik (685-705), were forced to lay siege to Mecca

and Medina to put down the dissident movement. During the assault the Ka'ba was burned, and for a long time the Umayyads had to live with the reproach of this impious act. The anti-caliph's reign ended with the surrender of the two rebellious holy cities, and he himself was put to death.

Despite their formidable military power, these Arabs who had annihilated the Sassanid empire and taken over the greater part of the Byzantine territories had produced no great art. Preoccupied as they were with their territorial expansion they had neglected the field of culture. But every powerful civilisation of those times called for an accompanying demonstration of artistic wealth, and the Gallic bishop Arculf, visiting Jerusalem in 670, was able to sneer at the sight of a "crudely-constructed building of great beams standing on ruins"; he was speaking of the primitive mosque which occupied the place where once the Temple of Jerusalem had stood. Compared with the masterpieces of Syro-Byzantine art at Busra, Damascus or Jerusalem, Islamic architecture half a century after the death of the Prophet was practically non-existent. In no way could the field mosques put up by the armies in Busra, Kufa or Fostat compare with the art of the Christian empire.

The Dome of the Rock: an octagon surmounted by a cupola originally in wood with a facing of gilded copper. The polychrome ceramic decoration above the marble lower section is an addition from the Ottoman period. Nearly 1,300 years old, and built by Abd al-Malik, the Dome of the Rock counts among the masterpieces of architectural history.

The Building of the Dome of the Rock

Jerusalem is the third holy city of Islam, after Mecca and Medina; here it was that Mohammed, on that famous "night journey" of which the Koran tells, was lifted up to heaven astride the Buraq to behold the face of God. Yet here stood nothing but a temporary construction! Nothing to commemorate with any splendour that vision over which the Archangel Gabriel had once presided when, from the sacred rock on which Abraham had sacrificed the lamb substituted for his son Isaac, the

Prophet had risen on his "night journey" to the very highest heavens! The Rock of Jerusalem where, as at the Ka'ba, the memory of Abraham was linked to that of the Prophet, deserved some glorification.

Given the situation in which rampant insurrection in Mecca and Medina prevented pilgrims from the Umayyad territories visiting those holy cities, the caliph Abd al-Malik set about the building of a sumptuous edifice in Jerusalem. This monument was to serve as a new place of pilgrimage for moslems, and also to eclipse the Byzantine Christian monuments such as the Basilica of the Holy Sepulchre in Jerusalem and the Church of the Nativity in Bethlehem. This work of art marking the beginnings of Islamic monumental architecture is the Dome of the Rock, crowning the esplanade where the Temple of Solomon had stood, destroyed by Nebuchadnezzar, rebuilt by Herod and razed again by Titus in 70 AD.

The programme was a complex one: it was not a question of building simply a mosque, a space intended for prayer (or prostration, as the Arab expression has it), but of a commemorative building crowning an

Overlooking the enclosing wall of the ancient Temple temenos at Jerusalem, the al-Aqsa mosque complements the Dome of the Rock to the south, and is topped by a silvered dome. Work of the Umayyad caliph al-Walid, "the Most Distant" was built between 705 and 709 AD.

important religious site. For this, the model of the mosque in the Prophet's house at Medina was not a helpful guide. What Abd al-Malik sought for the sacred rock at Jerusalem was a building suitable for the rite of circumambulation, as practiced around the Black Stone of the Ka'ba.

The architects the caliph commissioned for this great task were, like all his administrative and governmental entourage, Syro-Byzantines of Christian origin, who spoke Greek and kept up the traditions of the Antique world. They opted for a formula frequently used for such monuments in the Christian architecture of the first centuries AD: that of a martyrium, built around a central point with a circular ambulatory covered by a cupola, allowing pilgrims to circle the venerated place, whether it be a tomb, a relic or a sacred site.

In fact Abd al-Malik's realisation is exemplary in more than one way: just as the rich potentates of Petra had used the formal architectural language of the Greeks, just as those of Palmyra had surrounded themselves with imperial Roman monuments, and those of Hatra had combined Parthian forms with the Roman, the calif was not at all afraid to turn to a purely Byzantine artistic vocabulary, carried out by Syrian architects and mosaicists from Constantinople, for the construction of this first great Islamic sanctuary.

The building of the mosque lasted from 687 to 692. The outcome was an octagon enclosing two concentric ambulatories; the central circle around the sacred rock is covered by the superb cupola to which the building owes its name. This is not, oddly enough, built in stone, but has a double shell of wood, sheathed externally in gilded copper. The wooden cupola was a building technique typically Syrian in origin, going back to the Byzantine basilica of St. Simeon the Stylite (Qalat Seman) and the cathedral at Busra.

The dome is supported by a colonnade of sixteen arches resting on an alternation of one pillar to every three columns. A second colonnade, this time octagonal, surrounds it. This has a pillar at each corner alternating with two columns along each side, a total of twenty-four arches. The building has, in addition, four open gateways set at the four cardinal points in its octagonal outer wall.

The perfection and harmony of proportion in the Dome of the Rock derives from a plan based on a series of geometric and arithmetical formulae which make of it the concretisation of the esoteric mathematics of Antiquity. According to the Gnostics, whose ideas were based on the theories of the Platonists and Pythagoreans, numbers symbolise the macrocosm, and architecture thus reflects the laws of the universe. This is the antique conception incarnated in the Dome of the Rock at Jerusalem. Here one discovers, consciously or subconsciously, as one passes through the ambulatories, the whole spirit of the Ascetics based on the passage from square (the four gates) through octagon to circle (around the sacred rock)—a passage full of mystic symbolism.

It is a kind of "mandala" in which the pilgrim, through his circumambulation, has the concrete experience of squaring the circle, that is, the ascension from earth (square) to heaven (circle or dome), and the union of body and soul.

The magnificent antique column shafts in marble, granite and porphyry in a variety of colours are probably older works re-cycled; their gilded Corinthian capitals support arches with alternating black and white voussoirs. Apart from these structural elements, the monument is faced with sumptuous mosaics in the Byzantine style, representing vine shoots and branches springing up on a gold ground, acanthus plants and vases symbolically containing purifying water—symbols of immortality. This decoration is completed by a rich facing of marble, worked as a veneer with symmetrical veining, this too in a variety of colours.

Bottom:
Outcome of innumerable restorations and alterations, the al-Aqsa mosque in Jerusalem has seven aisles, the arcades running at right angles to the qibla. The style derives from Byzantine basilicas.

Above the bay leading to the mihrab in the al-Aqsa, this wooden cupola is supported by strange half-domes with hemi-spherical recesses above, decorated in mosaic.

Al-Walid the Builder

A year after the completion of the Dome of the Rock, Ibn al-Zubayr's insurrection was finally suppressed. Abd al-Malik's policy of turning Jerusalem into the centre of the Islamic world—a place of pilgrimage at the same time for Moslems, Jews and Christians—no longer had any object. The Ka'ba became once again the high place of Islam. His successor, the great al-Walid, who ruled the Umayyad empire from 705 to 715, was to complete the Dome of the Rock with the construction of the Al-Aqsa mosque on the same temple esplanade. He also endowed his capital at Damascus with an extraordinary and sumptuous mosque occupying the antique temenos, and had built, on the site of the Prophet's house at Medina (where Mohammed is also buried), a magnificent place of worship. This programme of prestigious projects, endowing the new moslem empire with monuments of its own, is again the work of craftsmen of Syro-Byzantine origin. They may even have been the same crafstmen as had worked on the Dome of the Rock.

Al-Walid launched this vast architectural programme while the empire was still in the full flood of its expansion. Under his caliphate, Samarkand and Bukhara became local seats of Arab government. The Islamic armies drove into Farghana and Chinese Turkestan. To the south-east, they invaded the Indus delta and entered Multan. At the far end of the Umayyad empire, the Arabs took a foothold in Spain, having already conquered Barbary (the Maghreb). In fact Tarik had disembarked in Gibraltar in 711 and by 714 the whole of Spain was under Arab control.

There is no doubt that Abd al-Malik's architects at the Dome of the Rock drew their inspiration from the rotunda of the Holy Sepulchre in Jerusalem itself, built in 335 by Constantine, and which also includes two concentric ambulatories. Al-Walid, however, in the building of the Al-Aqsa mosque, completed the parallel. Just as the Church of the Resurrection forms a whole with the Holy Sepulchre, towards the shrine of which its five aisles are aligned, so the Al-Aqsa mosque too presents a basilica-like plan oriented towards the Dome of the Rock. The two works are almost identical in their layout, with just one difference: while the Church of the Resurrection really is oriented towards the rotunda of the Holy Sepulchre, the Al-Aqsa, at the southern end of the esplanade, is oriented towards Mecca and *turns its back* on the Dome, although erected rigorously along the same axis.

The seven aisles of the Al-Aqsa, "the most distant" as the Koran calls it, have undergone many transformations in the course of the centuries. At the crossing of its principle aisle and the bay in front of the mihrab, the mosaics of vines, covering the vault and the corner pendentives, are in the same syle as those of the Dome of the Rock.

We have mentioned the mihrab, which constitutes in a way the holy of holies of every mosque: this is a niche in the qibla, the wall facing the worshippers as they pray; it indicates to the faithful the direction of Mecca, towards which they must prostrate themselves. For all the mihrabs in the Islamic world are oriented on Mecca, in a crown, as if drawn by some magnetism of the Black Stone.

At Medina, al-Walid, doubling the proportions of the mosque Mohammed had built in his own home, designed a quadrilateral with porticos around the central courtyard, forming hypostyles roofed with flat rafters.

View along the northern portico in the courtyard of the great mosque of the Umayyads, Damascus, built by al-Walid in 706-715. This section with its square pillars and stucco decoration is the result of 13th-century restoration work.

The Great Umayyad Mosque at Damascus

Al-Walid, leader of all the faithful, set out to endow Damascus, the Umayyad capital, with a place of worship worthy of the caliphate—an unequalled masterpiece. Even today, nearly twelve centuries after its construction and despite the terrible vicissitudes inflicted by time and by the hand of man, the Great Mosque of the Umayyads remains a glorious

monument. And the mystery of its genesis has never ceased to make the ink flow from the pens of specialists in Islamic art.

The edifice stands on the site of the old temenos of the Temple of Jupiter Damascene, which had been replaced in the 4th century by a great basilica consecrated to St. John the Baptist, commissioned by Theodosius (379-395). The mosque's proportions are considerable: 160 metres by 100 (175 yards by 110); the prayer hall, occupying the long southern side, is 136 metres wide by 40 (150 yards by 43) in depth—a wide but shallow space corresponding to the prayer hall (or haram), built of palm trunks and with a palm roof, in the first mosque at Medina. This hall consists of long wings on either side of a crossing with a high cupola above, in front of the mihrab. Each wing is divided into three aisles by the two colonnades down its length, their arcades lying parallel to the facade and the qibla. These great arcades, surmounted by smaller

The courtyard of the great Umayyad mosque in Damascus: the northern portico and, in front, the Treasury, an octagonal kiosk on eight antique columns, with magnificent mosaic work on a gold ground.

48

arches, two to each one of the arches on which they stand, are of powerful antique columns. All these colonnades, their two-tier rhythm echoed again in the porticos around the courtyard, have an air so Byzantine that many historians have argued that this is indeed the famous basilica of St. John, and that the caliph al-Walid had simply re-dedicated the same building to the islamic faith by changing the orientation of prayer, henceforth to be southwards, towards the Ka'ba, across the width of the building, instead of down its length towards the rising sun as in the already widespread tradition of Christian architecture.

I think myself that the truth is not as simple as that. The proportions of such a basilica would be totally incongruous: no Byzantine basilica is as long and narrow as this, and it is hard to see how the church dedicated to St. John the Baptist could have been erected along the southern wall of the temenos rather than at its centre. It seems far more likely, as indeed is born out by ancient texts referring to al-Walid's complete destruction of the Christian basilica, that what we have here is the re-use, on a grand scale, of material from the basilica. Seeing the architectural value of the magnificent arcades in the Byzantine basilica with its five

Facing page:
The interior of the great Umayyad mosque in Damascus. Two porticos parallel to the qibla divide the long wings of the sanctuary. The two tiers of Byzantine style arcades of Corinthian columns are probably recycled material from the basilica of St. John the Baptist built under Theodosius' reign.

aisles (as in the Church of the Resurrection in Jerusalem and of the Nativity in Bethlehem), the caliph's architects no doubt carefully dismantled the imposing structure, saving and numbering the columns to use them again in a new arrangement. Thus the four parallel arcades of the Byzantine church in the centre of the temenos, placed in pairs along its southern wall, became the two wings of a vast wide space. Islamic architecture frequently recycled elements from older structures, though generally on a smaller scale.

This said, such recycling in no way suggests a lack of respect for the antique works. On the contrary, in some instances it can be seen as a sign of the esteem in which they were held, just as authors turn to quotations from famous texts hoping to benefit from the veneration accorded to the sages they quote as authority. The Great Mosque at Damascus is a brilliant example: here, in this prime monument of the Islamic faith, St. John the Baptist is still venerated today, for a shrine has been dedicated to him at the very heart of the haram. The respect in which St. John, or

Largely restored after the disastrous fire of 1893, the mihrab in the mosque at Damascus, of remarkable richness and delicacy, combines Mamluk and Ottoman influences.

Above left:
Detail of the mosaic decoration in the Umayyad mosque in Damascus: a triumphal arch links two palaces in a garden of Paradise.

Yahya, is held goes back to Mohammed himself, who quotes him in the Koran.

On the interior faces of the walls around the antique temenos, and on the porticos bordering the mosque's courtyard on the north, east and west sides, as well as on the principal facade of the prayer hall, one can still see remnants of mosaics. This sumptuous facing which once decorated all the visible surfaces of the building must have constituted the vastest ensemble of mosaic work of all its epoque. Of purely Byzantine manufacture, the decoration was carried out by 1200 Greek craftsmen or so, we are told by Ibn Battutah.

The theme of these great murals, made up of millions of small coloured glass cubes, is mainly living plants—trees, bushes, foliage—with castles and aquatic palaces, villas and summerhouses, arbours and bridges scattered amid the greenery. All this decor of cool shadow traced out on a gold background is treated according to Romano-Byzantine artistic conventions, creating wide landscapes in which the human figure appears nowhere at all.

As to the meaning of these pastoral scenes, they are in fact a representation of the Garden of Paradise as promised to the faithful by the

Ruins of the Umayyad city of Anjar in the Lebanon, built in the time of al-Walid on a layout that drew directly on Roman town planning.

The little fortress of Khasr Kharana in the Jordanian desert follows the classic lines of a Roman frontier fortification. This Umayyad work beside a wadi must have been the centre of an irrigated agricultural holding.

Above right:
Vaulted hall in the Umayyad "castle" of Khasr Kharana, its roofing owing much to Sassanid forms, especially the large arches resting on pillars like bundles of small columns.

Facing page, bottom:
Detail of frescoes from the Khasr Amra: workers carrying stone blocks for the construction of the Umayyad "palace". These figurative paintings must date back to the reign of al-Walid, and are an interesting example of classical Arab art.

Koran: the greenery, the living waters and the sumptuous dwellings are simply a conception of the Garden of Eden to which the Prophet refers again and again, and their presence in the mosque is to tell the faithful of the happiness they may earn by a full obedience to the Koran.

Palaces and Cities of the Umayyads

At the same time as these luxurious religious monuments were being built, the Umayyad caliphs were also carrying through an important programme in the field of secular architecture. Here too it was the Romano-Byzantine tradition that was to be followed, both in town planning and in the building of their "desert palaces".

Thus the Umayyad town of Anjar on the Bekaa plain near Baalbeck in the Lebanon, built between 714 and 715 at the end of al-Walid's reign, is laid out on the Roman plan of the "urbs quadrata" or square town, its enclosing wall marked out at intervals by towers and its two colonnaded avenues, the cardo and the decumanus, crossing at right angles under a four-arched triumphal arch, dividing the town into equal quarters.

The great vaulted hall of the Umayyad "palace" of Khasr Amra, in fact a bath complex standing in the Jordanian desert near the wadi Butm. Three parallel barrel vaults supported by two large arches 6 metres (6.5 yards) across cover an "audience hall" decorated by frescoes of great interest.

The austere exterior of the Khasr Amra with its vaults and cupolas above walls kept almost blank to keep out the desert heat.

In the heart of the sandy wastes of Jordan and Syria stand palaces long regarded as the "follies" of sovereigns avid to return to the desert from which they came, to go hunting with falcons. We now know that they are in fact huge "villas" in the Roman sense, agricultural establishments where the owners of huge estates would devote themselves to growing wheat, fruit and even sugar cane, thanks to intensive irrigation by means of a skilful irrigation system stretching across huge domains such as at Mshatta, Khirbet al-Mafjar, Kasr Amra or Kasr Kharana.

The paradox is the adoption of defensive forms and systems, both for cities and palaces, along the lines of Roman forward camps, on this eastern frontier once guarded by the legions. For in fact the Parthian and Sassanid threat was no longer any more than a memory in this Islamic empire which had just reached its farthest limits: in 716 the caliph Sulayman laid siege to Constantinople again, without succeeding in seizing it: at the far end of the Mediterranean an expedition by the prefect of Spain was halted before Poitiers by Charles Martel: at Talas, the Moslems defeated the Chinese on the Syr-Darya, but did not progress any further east. The age of the great expansion was over. A century after the death of the Prophet, the Arab world stretched from the Atlantic right to the Chinese frontier.

The Great Abbassid Empire

The end of the Umayyad dynasty is a dark drama of assassination, full of sound and fury. The last of the Umayyad caliphs was Marwan II, who came to power in 744. He moved his residence to Harran in Mesopotamia to be closer to the centre of the revolts which had broken out in northern Iran. But the caliph was to be defeated by insurgent troops in 750. From Iraq he fled to Egypt, but there he was assassinated, at the same time as all the members of the Umayyad family who had ruled the empire for ninety years. Only one escaped, the Umayyad who founded the independent emirate of Cordoba in Spain (756-1031). One of his successors, Abd al-Rahman III, proclaimed himself caliph in 929 and thus drew Spain even further from Abbassid control.

The "Round City" of al-Mansur

It was the Alids on one hand and Abu Muslim on the other who had revolted in Khurasan in Iran and who favoured the accession of the Abbassids, a branch of Mohammed's family, to the throne. Abu al-Abbas, who was proclaimed caliph at Kufa in Lower Mesopotamia, came to be called al-Saffah, the Bloody. With his accession came the decline of Graeco-Byzantine influences in the caliph's court, in favour of the ways of thought of the ancient Persian and Mesopotamian civilisations. But the partisans of Shiism who had contributed to the establishment of the new dynasty were frustrated in their hopes one day to accede to power.

For from then on the Abbassid caliphate remained tied to Sunnite orthodoxy.

After the short-lived establishment of the Abbassids at Kufa, the caliph al-Mansur (754-775) established his capital at Bagdad, to the north of the ancient Sassanid capital of Ctesiphon and not far from Seleucia on the Tigris. He built it on a circular plan in the Partho-Sassanid tradition, like Hatra. This was the famous "round city", known throughout the world, although today no vestige of it remains. For Bagdad was built of brick—mostly unbaked—and was besieged and taken by storm several times.

The town was entirely surrounded by a dry moat, and within that a triple surrounding wall, the outermost measuring 2.6 kilometres (1.6 mile) in circumference. This much we know from the ample descriptions of this sumptuous city left to us by Arab writers. Four fortified gates opened up, at the north-east, north-west, south-east and south-west, in the directions of Arabia, Syria, Kirman and Khurasan. And on the axial roads between the gates stood huge bazaars with no less than eighty arcades on either side of the axial roads. The city's quarters within the

Below left:
The porticos of heavy round pillars and tierce-point arches around the courtyard of the small palace mosque of Ukhaydir.

surrounding walls were laid out radially. The whole centre of this "round city" was occupied by huge gardens, 1500 metres (1640 yards) in diameter, at the heart of which stood the caliph's palace and its adjoining great mosque.

This gigantic palace, covering an area about 200 metres (220 yards) square, included at the heart of the buildings a throne room in the form of an "iwan". This huge roofed construction, open along its facade, its origin going back to a Persian tradition highly developed in the Sassanid period, probably drew its inspiration from the great iwan of the Palace of Ctesiphon whose arch rose in one sweep to a height of 36 metres (120 feet) and spanned over 27 metres (30 yards). As with the Sassanids, the function of this edifice was to be a throne room for the Abbassids, where the caliph received his guests and suppliants with a pomp and luxury never known before.

Beside the palace stood the mosque, on a square plan, its sides measuring 100 metres (110 yards) and thus enclosing one hectare. It had a great central courtyard surrounded by porticos, with a hypostyle prayer hall. In 808, this first Bagdad mosque was demolished by Harun

Looking down the reception halls, Ukhaydir palace: a complex system of vaulting on powerful masonry columns without capitals.

Facing page, top:
Western entrance to the fortified enceinte around the royal residence at Ukhaydir, not far from the ancient Babylon, built in 778 in the Abbassid period.

Facing page, bottom:
The formidable fortified enceinte of the Ukhaydir palace: round towers punctuate a curtain wall bearing machicolations, arrow slits and a wall-walk in the upper part.

al-Rashid who rebuilt it entirely in baked brick with a revetment of carved plaster. Then in 873 the caliph al-Mutadid enlarged his predecessor's construction, building an extension on the other side of the palace wall onto which the first qibla backed, so doubling the building's surface area. The result was an immense edifice 200 metres long by 100 in depth (220 yards by 110).

The Palace of Ukhaydir

The oldest of the monuments of the Abbassid period which has survived to our day is the palace of Ukhaydir. Paradoxically this is not a brick construction as were so many of the Mesopotamian works, following a tradition of brickwork dating back to the Sumerians, and which indeed was obligatory, given the total absence of building stone in this region of alluvial plains. The fortress at Ukhaydir could be built in stone owing to the fact that the site lies beyond the plains of Mesopotamia properly speaking, in a region with a rock bed, to the south-west of ancient Babylon.

Built of large stone blocks embedded in concrete, this huge palace dating back to 778 covers a rectangular area 175 metres by 170 (190 yards by 185) as defined by its outer wall; the inner wall, which encloses the greater part of the palace buildings, reaches 112 metres by 82 (122 yards by 90). The fortress is additionally surrounded in its entirety by an external ring of defenses covering 33 hectares (80 acres). The defensive walls of the palace are powerfully fortified: round defensive towers furnished with arrow-slits punctuate the curtain wall. Between the towers the walls are surmounted by twin overhanging arcades supporting the wall-walk, and providing an original system of machicolations. Within the enceinte, instead of standing at the centre of the enclosure the palace buildings are ranged along its northern wall.

Behind the principal entry along the northern wall, one finds an

Facing page:
Known as the Malwiyah, the Spiral, this fantastic helical minaret, 55 metres (180 feet) high, overlooks the great mosque at Samarra, built between 848 and 852 by the Abbassid caliph al-Mutawakkil. The brickwork architecture takes its inspiration from Babylonian ziggurats.

View from the top of the Malwiyah: the now empty 4-hectare (10-acre) enclosure of the great mosque at Samarra. A hypostyle hall and porticos around a courtyard once occupied the space.

Detail of sculptured plaster facing from the great Abbassid caliph's palace at Samarra (Bagdad Museum).

Above left:
The enclosure wall of the great Samarra mosque, punctuated by towers. Enclosing the biggest mosque in the world, it measures 240 metres by 156 (260 yards by 170).

enormous vaulted hall forming the vestibule, with a four-centred vault as its ceiling resting on each side on an arcade supported by four solid pillars in the form of cylindrical columns, but engaged in the side walls. This vestibule recalls the spatial formulae of the Roman era in the west with its subtle buttressing techniques. From here one enters the main courtyard, measuring 35 metres by 28 (38 yards by 30); it is around this court that the private quarters are arranged, all designed on the same repetitive plan. The north-west corner of the palace also includes a little palace mosque which has not been oriented. This, with a courtyard bordered by powerful arches on round pillars, served as the prince's oratory. In fact Ukhaydir was built by Isa ibn Musa, a nephew of al-Mansur, who made an attempt at the caliphate but was ousted. He retired to his own landholding where he developed a rich agriculture like that of the desert palaces of Syria and Jordan in the time of the Umayyads.

Samarra, the New Capital

After Harun al-Rashid, Abbassid power fell to al-Mamun, son of the caliph and of a Persian concubine. For a while al-Mamun ruled from the town of Merv, to the north of Khurasan (between Afghanistan and the Aral Sea), before returning to Bagdad and making that his capital city. This brought renewed hope to the Alid population, for al-Mamun surrounded himself with Persian courtiers. The caliph even went so far as to appoint as his successor a descendant of Hussein, Ali al-Rida, who lived in Medina. But Ali was assassinated during his voyage to Merv, and once more the reconciliation between the Sunnite Abbassids and the Alids fell through.

Remarkable as the design of the "Round City" of Bagdad was, the arrangement in a circle of its peripheral districts and the siting of the palace at its centre soon presented major inconveniences. It was the growing importance of the Turkish praetorian guard with whom the caliphs had surrounded themselves since the days of al-Mamun and al-Mutasin that demonstrated the problems of this layout. For their were growing tensions between this personal guard of the caliph and the Arab and Persian population of Bagdad, and the structure of the town did not allow for the restriction of the turbulent and pugnacious Turkish troops to the outskirts: they had to be kept close to the caliph to defend him against a population always ready to riot.

Faced with ever-increasing incidents between Arabo-Persians and the Turkish military, the caliph Mutasin was obliged to transfer the capital of his empire to Samarra, also situated on the Tigris, but about a hundred kilometers (60 miles) to the north-west of Bagdad. He carried out this transfer in 836 AD. His town planners, bearing in mind the practical necessities, opted for a plan in which a number of installations such as palaces, living quarters, mosques, garrisons and administrative centres each formed its own walled unit, these dotted along the river bank. This conurbation, today entirely in ruins, in the end stretched along 25 kilometres (15 miles) of the river and counted several hundred thousand inhabitants—this at a time when the population of Paris, for example, was 30,000 and London much smaller! The Samarra of the Abbassids must have been, in the 9th century, one of the most populous cities in the world.

All that is left of this capital city is barely-recognisable remains, for all its architecture was built, after the Mesopotamian tradition, in unbaked brick, with facings of baked brick reserved for the most important buildings and the show-pieces. These also bore stucco revetments, finely chiselled.

This vast administrative, military and religious centre (the caliph being the head of all the faithful), endowed with hippodromes, huge bazaars, craftsmen's and tradesmen's quarters, with its docks along the river, obviously contained immense palace complexes.

The portico of the Ibn Tulun mosque: pointed, slightly horse-shoed arches and pillars framed by colonnettes.

One of the porticos in the Ibn Tulun mosque in Cairo: built in plastered brick and with flat raftered ceilings, the building offers fine perspectives giving an impression of serenity and spaciousness.

The Balkuwara for example, built by al-Mutawakkil in 850, stretches along 450 metres (490 yards) and was developed symmetrically around an axis 800 metres (870 yards) long. It was a veritable imperial walled city with its succession of gardens and its series of gateways leading to the heart of the palace, where the courtyard, surrounded by buildings, opened out onto the royal iwan, followed by audience rooms and grand halls, the whole perspective focussing on a terrace overlooking the river bank.

Big as a whole town, the principal mosque of this capital of the Abbassids is one of the most impressive buildings of Arab Islamic art, despite the incomplete state in which we find it today. It is also the biggest mosque in the moslem world. Constructed between 848 and 852 it is composed of an immense fortified surrounding wall 240 metres by 156 (262 yards by 170), this surrounded in turn by an exterior enclosure 440 metres by 376 (480 yards by 411), outlining the space consecrated to prayer, in the manner of the "temenos" of antiquity.

The baked brick wall includes fourty-four defensive towers at intervals around it. Inside, the 4-hectare (ten-acre) space which today lies empty once comprised a courtyard surrounded on three sides by porticos on three rows of pillars, the fourth side making a gigantic hypostyle. Altogether there were 216 pillars supporting a flat raftered roof of teak.

Opposite the qibla, outside the enclosure itself but placed on the longitudinal axis of the building, stands a fantastic minaret, a strange spiral structure 55 metres (160 feet) high. This minaret, from which the muezzin once called the faithful to prayer, is called Malwiyah, the Spiral. Reminiscent of the legendary Tower of Babel, it must have been inspired by the Babylonian ziggurats, but adapted to a circular plan. Such a return to Mesopotamian sources demonstrates the continuity between Arab works and those of their antecedents going right back to an age two thousand years earlier.

The brilliant city which was Samarra, its planning a reflection of the breadth of vision of the masters of the Abbassid dynasty, was nevertheless abandoned in 883, less than fifty years after its construction. The caliphs returned to Bagdad, where they fell under the sway of the Turkish praetorian guard and the Shiite viziers who took control of both the finances and the state power, although they retained the fiction of an elected caliph.

The immense Abbassid empire began to decline from the mid 9th century, although the dynasty continued right up to the mid 13th century. Its fragmentation began with the revolt of the Karmats of Syria and Arabia and the insurrection of the Saffarids of Seistan and Khurasan. Then the general Ahmed ibn Tulun, Turkish in origin but born in Samarra, and whom the caliph had appointed governor of Egypt, declared independence in 868. The empire disintegrated slowly. Nationalist developments were to lead to the real collapse of the empire in the 10th century with the secession of the Fatimids in Egypt, the Umayyads in Cordoba who proclaimed themselves caliphs, and the Buwayhids in the south of Persia. Finally the Samanids succeeded the Saffarids and from their base at Bukhara ruled over their own powerful emirate.

From Egypt to Tunisia

Ibn Tulun's origins explain the style of the mosque, clearly influenced by those at Samarra, that this independent ruler of Egypt had built in his capital city of Fostat (Cairo). Here one finds the building techniques of brick and chiselled plaster characteristic of the Mesopotamian works, as well as the spiral minaret. Built between 876 and 879, this huge mosque, covering a square 162 metres (177 yards) along each side, has a square courtyard enclosed on three sides by porticos with double arcades, and on the fourth by a hypostyle prayer hall with five bays. All the supporting pillars are surmounted by large pointed arches.

Also dating from the reign of Ibn Tulun, the Nilometer of Roda at Cairo bears witness to the importance of water supplies in the moslem world. For here the fertility of the soil, and thence the tax rates, depended on the level of the Nile in flood. The Nilometer is a deep square pit at the centre of which rises a graduated column, and it was based on a design by the famous Arab mathematician al-Farghani. The walls around the underground pit, in fine dressed limestone, are reinforced by tierce-point arches surmounting niches on each side.

Cairo also offers a lovely hypostyle mosque which bears the name of the conqueror of Egypt, Amr' ibn al-Ass. It was built at Fostat in 642, then rebuilt in 698 and in 711, extended in 750 and 791, and reached its present dimensions in 827. Its structure, based on 150 columns of which most, like the capitals, are re-cycled antiques, makes use of very lightly pointed arches lying at right angles to the qibla. It is a formula which has produced a light and spacious hall.

This type of hypostyle mosque on antique columns can be found again at Qayrawan and at Cordoba. In the city of Qayrawan (the Encampment) which was to become the capital of Ifriqiyah, the mosque was founded by an Aghlabid prince in 836, and many times restored since then. This mosque can be counted among the most harmonious works of classical Islam in the west. It offers an impressive square minaret of a type which was to spread throughout the Maghreb and into Spain.

We should point out also, in the same city, the remarkable work represented by two basins built as reservoirs for irrigation. These circular reservoirs with reinforced walls, the larger of the two 128 metres (140 yards) in diameter, are still in use today, over a thousand years after their installation.

Bottom:
The great mosque of Qayrawan was founded in 836, but the hypostyle prayer hall with its recycled antique columns dates for the most part from 862-863, and bears a resemblance to that in the Amr in Cairo.

These two circular basins, built as reservoirs by the Aghlabids of Qayrawan in 875, are still in use in that ancient capital of Ifriqiyah.

From the Fatimids to the Crusades

For three centuries, the Arab empire had taught the Moslem world to speak the language of the Koran. Arabic was imposed along with the moslem religion up to the farthest frontiers reached by the caliphs' troops. It held sway from the Atlantic to the Chinese border. But from then on, the awakening of national minorities and the massive conversion of new tribes in central Asia was to produce a weakening of its influence. For one must realise that the Arabic which spread across the conquered territories was in fact the native language of a relatively small population (the Arabs of Arabia around the year 500 counted no more than two or three million), and it was a language which, prior to the Koran, had produced only a limited literature. Arabic replaced on the one hand, in the Byzantine provinces, the Greek "koïne" which was spoken in common with Aramaic in Syria and Palestine, and with Coptic in Egypt, and on the other hand, in the regions of Iran, Pahlavi or middle Persian, which was the spoken language there while oriental Aramaic served as the language of commerce and diplomacy. In the 10th

على شاطيء النهر وصورة البني فوق البئر فوقه عليهن ونثر به
ومما جاء بجستان من هما نير بهن نهر التزار بـ

19

فقال ازكز لديج حتى مع عينيه وقام على نفسه ومؤمنه
بين المشئت وجمه وقلت له لا با به عليه رحمد الله ما جعل فرجعه
عند كانت واجرمن الوجه لا تخص فقال لي عندما سمع عذل معزوره

Miniature from "The Story of Bayad and Riyad", dating from the 13th century and showing a "noria", the irrigation wheel used by the Arabs.

One of these great wheels built to raise water from the river into irrigation canals still stands in the city of Hama on the Orontes river in Syria. Irrigation canals carried water long distances across country.

century, the language of Persia began to develop anew, as is shown by "nationalist" works like those of Firdawsi. In the century that followed, the penetration of the Seljuks, partisans of Sunnite Islam, imposed the use of the Turkish language in Anatolia. And in the India of the 16th century, the Mongols favoured the language belonging to the military rulers of that country: Urdu, a mixture of Arabic and Persian which was used throughout the Mongolian empire and which has remained in Pakistan.

Arabic thus remained the basic language from the shores or the Atlantic (and throughout North Africa, where it had ousted latin) to the Mesopotamian delta, where it stopped at the foot of the Zagros mountains, and to the gates of Cilicia where it gave way to Turkish. But even within the area which is henceforth that of the Arab world, despite a common unifying language, the political cohesion of the Abbassid empire could not be maintained. We need only recall the secession of Egypt in the time of the Tulunids, who cut the empire's contact with North Africa and pulled the whole of the moslem West out of Bagdad's control.

The Rise of the Fatimids

As the break-up of the Abbassid empire was accentuated, it was essentially the Mediterranean Middle East, with Egypt and Syria, which took the lead in the cultural movement among the Arab countries. In this region of Islam, the Shiites conferred authority on Ubaydullah al-Mahdi, a descendent of Ali and of Fatima, the Prophet's daughter. They

Facing page, top:
Silk samite fabric from the Fatimid period, with motifs inspired by Sassanid designs. A 9th century work from Egypt, it demonstrates the progress made in weaving techniques in the Islamic period (Abegg Foundation, Riggisberg).

Facing page, bottom:
Fatimid linen fabric from the workshops of the royal court of Lower Egypt, dating from the 9th century. The complexity of the motifs and dyes attained in the Tiraz, the workshops of the caliphate, is remarkable (Abegg Foundation, Riggisberg).

61

Founded in 970 by the Fatimids of Cairo, the al-Azhar mosque, religious centre of this Shiite caliphate, later became the Koranic university of orthodox Sunnism.

The hypostyle prayer hall of the al-Azhar mosque, Cairo: recycled antique columns in arcades running parallel to the qibla, interrupted only where the two arcades of the triumphal aisle up to the mihrab cut across at right angles.

founded an Alid dynasty in North Africa; the Fatimids were in power in Ifriqiyah from 906, then took power in Egypt in 969 and in Damascus in 970.

A large part of the Moslem world seemed to shift over to the Alid side. This religious movement was destined above all to check the caliph of Bagdad, whose yoke the people hoped to throw off. In the east of the empire, the Buwayhids and Samanids reflected the tendency developing in the west and imposed Alid power across a wide area. In Bagdad itself, the caliph became a puppet of the Buwayhid emirs. But Sunnite orthodoxy received unexpected help from the Turks, who had traditionally been devoted defenders of the caliph. From the depths of central Asia, the Seljuks went on the march. In 1055 they seized the city of Bagdad, having already subdued Persia. Then in 1071 they forced on into Anatolia where they founded the sultanate of Rum, and in 1079 they even seized Jerusalem.

So the equilibrium was maintained between the two branches of Islam. But from the 10th century on, the caliph at Bagdad was no longer

anything but a religious symbol. And in Cairo the Fatimids hastened to elect an anti-caliph. They developed, in addition, a brilliant culture full of innovation in the new capital they built beside Fostat.

The Foundation of Cairo

The Fatimid current in Egypt endowed this country of the Nile with a remarkable civilising impulse that lasted for two centuries. The foundation of Cairo (al-Khaira, the Victorious) was the work of the general Gauwar, commander of the Fatimid caliph al-Muizz' troops. The city rose between the river and the limestone chain of the Mokkatam which overlooks it, not far from Babylon, the ancient Graeco-Roman and later Coptic town, and not far from Fostat.

The town plan was that of a fortress acting as "forbidden city", reserved for the sovereign, his court and his administrative personnel, and watched over by his praetorian guard. Here were situated the treasury, the mint, the library, the arsenal, and mausoleums. The city was surrounded by a square brick fortified wall, over a kilometre (0.62 mile) square; at its centre stood the famous al-Azhar mosque. The foundation of this great Koranic school, dates back to 970. But the extensions and modifications carried out over the thousand years of its existence have somewhat altered the form of the original building. Al-Azhar (the Splendid) is, within the tradition of Ibn Tulun and Ibn al-Ass, a courtyard mosque with a surrounding portico. Most of the columns are re-

used antiques, and they are surmounted by stilted arches with sharply curved shoulders and a taut slope above, a style that was to become a classic in Egypt and has been called erroneously the "Persian arch". As at the Ibn al-Ass, these arches are inter-connected by tiebeams, but here the bays are formed by arcades running parallel to the qibla. In addition, a triumphal alley wider than the other aisles leads to the mihrab, following a formula that appeared at Qayrawan.

It should not be forgotten that the al-Azhar mosque was first conceived as a Shiite sanctuary, before becoming the principal university of Sunnism after the fall of the Fatimids.

The Fatimid caliphs Muizz and Aziz, with their religious toleration, turned largely to Coptic craftsmen whose contribution to the rise of the city was an important one. The Copts also occupied important administrative posts. But the coming of Hakim led to persecution of the Christians from 996 on. The Alid caliph prescribed a rigid religious asceticism and tried to impose a very puristic Islam. At one angle of the capital's enceinte he had built a vast mosque inspired by the works of Ibn Tulun. This building carries powerful minarets rising above pylon-shaped towers. Little remains of the huge building within its perimeter wall but the still imposing ruins of arcades which remind one of the glory of Cairo's Fatimid period, when the caliph Hakim proclaimed himself a god and was worshipped as such...

In the decades that followed, the Egyptian anti-caliphs had increasing difficulty in imposing their authority. The praetorian guard increasingly imposed its own will on its supposed master. Under al-Mustansir, who remained on the throne for over fifty years without ever really ruling, disorder grew into a state of anarchy. In 1074 al-Mustansir, trying to re-establish order in his ruined country, called for help on an Armenian, Badr Gamali, who had sought refuge in Egypt together with his troops after their defeat in 1071 by the Seljuks at Mantzikart.

But, with the strength of this rabble of soldiery, Badr sequestered the caliph in the palace. He had his troops—accompanied as they were by architects and engineers—build a new fortified wall around Cairo, with monumental gates of which three remain almost intact to this day— Bab al-Nasr, Bab al-Futuh and Bab al-Zawilah. They date from between 1087 and 1091 and are typical works of these Syro-Armenian emigrés who, coming as they did from Edessa, were heirs to Romano-Byzantine military architecture.

The Age of the Crusades

In this period a new element appeared in the Middle East with the crusaders, who seized Edessa in 1097, Antioch and Damascus in 1098 and Jerusalem in 1099. The establishment of a Latin Kingdom of Jerusalem the same year gave the Christians a territory in Palestine which was to be maintained until 1187, when the crusaders were defeated at Hattin and Saladin retook Jerusalem. But a Christian presence in the area was maintained right up to the fall of St. John of Acre in 1291.

Between the 10th and 13th centuries, then, the region saw a period of great turbulence, characterised by armed confrontation but also by a fruitful contact between Christians and Moslems. Emulation was lively and exchanges grew. The art of the siege made tremendous progress as can be seen in the great military defence works in Damascus and Aleppo on the Moslem side, or in the Krak des Chevaliers and many other Christian Frankish castles in the Holy Land, which provide examples of a formidable military architecture.

Apart from this intermittent war, there was an intensive commercial exchange. Medieval Europe became avid for Eastern produce—spices and aromatics which the Arab merchants procured, and also craftwork such as brocades and fine fabrics, damascened weapons, delicately-worked leather. Luxuries re-appeared in the ports and merchant cities of the Middle Ages in Italy and the south of France after the period of terrible scarcity the medieval world had lived through, with a lack of workable metals and no international trade.

Saladin and the Ayyubids

Although the Fatimids of Cairo had conquered Syria in 988, the united destiny of the two countries did not last long under their aegis. The intervention by the Seljuks upset the Alids' schemes, and the arrival of the crusaders then added further to the confusion; Christian troops even launched an expedition against Egypt in 1116.

Resistance in Kurdistan under the emirs of Mossul continued to grow until Saladin (Salah al-Din) made his appearance, first as prefect of Alexandria, then as prime minister of a Syrian general fighting the Alid caliph on behalf of Nur al-Din, ruler of Damascus. In 1167, Cairo fell. But the end of the anti-caliphate in 1171, instigated by Saladin, passed almost unnoticed in the upheavals that came with the wars between Moslems and Christians. In 1183 a state was established unifying Egypt, Syria, Mesopotamia and the Yemen under the Ayyubid dynasty (Saladin's father, of Kurdish origin, was called Ayyub and ruled at Baalbeck). It was this Arab coalition, fighting under the flag of the caliph of Bagdad, which defeated the crusaders at Hattin. But on Saladin's death the vast territories he had controlled were once again split up into a number of smaller sultanates.

In 1206, a little over a century after the fortifications of Cairo had been rebuilt, the city of Damascus in turn was endowed with a fortified wall around its citadel. It was a rectangular enceinte punctuated by twelve square towers built of large cut stone blocks "en bosse", with batteries of machicolations overhanging externally, held up by corbels.

Facing page top:
Facade of the small al-Akhmar mosque, Cairo, built by the Fatimids in 1125. Stalactite or mukarna motifs of Persian origin make their appearance: they were to take an important place in Islamic art.

Facing page, bottom:
The Abbassid caliphs' mausoleum, in Cairo, was built about 1242 and housed the spoils of war of these descendents of the Abbassids of Bagdad.

Detail of the prayer hall, Sali Talai mosque, Cairo, founded by the Fatimids in 1160. A flat raftered ceiling is supported by tall stuccoed arches on antique columns, the arcades running parallel to the qibla.

In the same period Aleppo too, in northern Syria, fortified its citadel. This castle, crowning a rocky hill which with a sharply sloping "glacis" of paving stones all round took on a conical form, dominates the medieval town from some 50 metres (150 feet) up. The great natural mound on which the town had been concentrated in the first milennium BC was soon unable to hold all the population, and from the time of Antiquity the town had spread around the foot of its imposing acropolis. In 1209 the Ayyubid al-Ghazi replaced the old Byzantine fortress with a new construction. This, devastated by the Mongols in 1258 was rebuilt in 1292, destroyed anew by Tamerlane and again restored in the 16th century. But considerable portions of the 13th century structure can still be seen; the bartizan with its sloping causeway over the moat and leading to a projecting barbican must count among the most imposing works of medieval military architecture in the Middle East. Here one can see the same kind of machicolations as at Damascus.

The Sunnite Madrasas

The reign of Saladin had ensured the return of Sunnism in force. Like the Seljuks, the Ayyubid dynasty showed itself to be a powerful protector of orthodoxy. This is why the primary religious buildings of the period are its madrasas, the Koranic schools. And it is here that one sees the development of an architectural style making frequent use of the iwan—for this originally Persian building form, a covered and sheltered space fully open onto a courtyard, is ideally suited to the requirements of teaching.

The most remarkable of these schools of the Ayyubid period is at Aleppo—the Firdaws Madrasa, or madrasa of Paradise, built in 1233 on the south side of the town by the widow of al-Ghazi. Built throughout in magnificent dressed stone, the madrasa is composed of a central courtyard surrounded on three sides by porticos with tierce-point arches resting on columns. Onto the fourth side opens a great rectangular iwan with a pointed arch. At the centre of the courtyard stands a basin for ritual ablutions just as one finds in Persian mosques. And the high entrance gateway is surmounted by a niche encrusted with decorations in

the form of stalactites, or mukarnas, these too Iranian in origin, their first appearance in the Middle East being in the lovely square vault of the Maristan Nuri at Damascus, built in 1154, where a formula originally treated in brickwork had been translated into stone. The change of medium, it should be stressed, required the development of great skill in stereotomy, the mason's science of cut stone. We may add too that this stalactite motif also reappears in the capitals atop the columns in the Firdaws Madrasa. Finally there is the magnificent paving of geometric motifs in contrasting black and white marble, contributing to the overall effect of this Syrian monument of religious art as a masterpiece of serenity and quietude.

Architecture in Bagdad

One region where Persian influence was the norm is certainly Mesopotamia. It was after all, with Ctesiphon, the heart of the Sassanid empire. And indeed the 12th and 13th century monuments of Bagdad reflect very well the intensity of the interchange between Arabs and Persians. This is as much the case in the caliph's mansion known as the Abbassids' Palace as in the Koranic school called the al-Mustansiriyah Madrasa: both are brick-built in the tradition that goes back through the works of classical Islam to the very roots of Mesopotamian architecture.

The Abbassids' palace, built by the caliph Nasir al-Din Allah (1180-

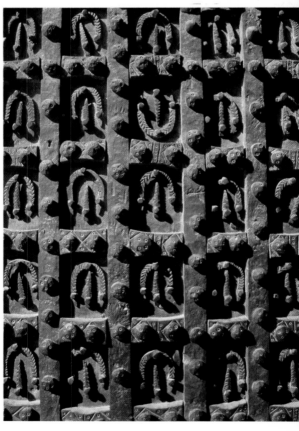

The Maristan Nuri in Damascus, the hospital built in 1154 by Nur al-Din: here, a stalactite stonework cupola. The treatment of the Seljuk stalactite motif in finely cut stone was to spread throughout the Moslem world from Cairo to Mongolian India.

General view of the Firdaws Madrasa, or Paradise Madrasa, at Aleppo, built in 1233. Pure forms, bare walls, stone cupolas.

Above right:
Decoration of the mihrab in the Firdaws Madrasa—a skilful play of interlacing in polychrome marble.

1225), comprises a courtyard surrounded on all four sides by arcades dominated by two central iwans on its longitudinal axis. As in Persia, these iwans must have served as throne rooms before the building was converted into a madrasa, when they were used as classrooms. As to the arcades, they are honeycombed with small concave triangles, the small scale of which shows that they are a purely decorative adaptation of the structural formula used in Persia by the Seljuks. This decoration of stalactites (mukarnas) was to become classic throughout medieval and late Islamic architecture, reaching Egypt, the Maghreb and Spain, and found in some buildings of Mongol India. It took on very varied forms, was worked in a whole range of different media from brick to ceramic tilework and from stone to plaster on a wooden frame.

Al-Mustansiriyah, built by one of the last Abbassid caliphs stripped of all temporal power, owes its name to al-Mustansir who ruled from 1226 to 1241. The Persian design with four iwans appears again here with great authority: this madrasa, with its fountain in the centre of the courtyard where the great apses of the iwans open out, is built in a very elongated form along the bank of the Tigris in the heart of Bagdad. To compensate visually for the length of the courtyard, the architect has subtly adopted a design that adds smaller secondary iwans on either side of the central iwans in the long arcades. One thus has three apses side by side breaking into the rhythm of the two tiers of arcades around the courtyard—two tiers as in the Abbassid palace.

The Art of the Weaver

Among the arts at which Egypt and Syria particularly excelled in the Fatimid and Ayyubid period, one must mention textiles. The creation of new types of weave—brocades, damask, samite—and original motifs took on considerable importance in the craftwork of the period. The Fatimids were heirs to the Coptic skills in this technology, and we know the beauty of Coptic fabrics found in the tombs of Fayyum, Alexandria and Thebaid. But the Arab weavers further refined their predecessors' techniques and developed increasingly sophisticated looms.

Linen, wool, cotton and silk fabrics flowed from the workshops of the caliph's court, the Tiraz, supplying the caliph and his high dignitaries with the robes of office that showed the wearer's rank. These sovereigns had developed a custom of distributing "robes of honour" made in the court workshops.

Detail of double corner-capital with stalactite motifs decorating the Firdaws Madrasa in Aleppo. Note the wooden bearing between capital and arch, a survival from Byzantine building techniques.

Portico and courtyard in the Firdaws Madrasa, with its large tierce-point arches supported on columns with stalactite capitals. Around the ablution fountain at the centre, a superb coloured pavement with a severe geometric design.

Detail of the chiselled brick decoration of the Mustansiriyah Madrasa built in Bagdad between 1226 and 1241 by the caliph al-Mustansir.

Bottom:
The tomb of Zubaydah, Bagdad, topped by its curious cupola: the convex shapes form stalactites on the interior. Dating from the 13th century, this symmetrical octagonal building makes implicit reference to the Dome of the Rock.

The courtyard of the Mustansiriyah in Bagdad, with its double arcades punctuated by large iwans of Persian inspiration.

Miniatures and Manuscripts

It is all too often believed that painting was a non-existent art in the Arab world, and yet, particularly during the 13th century, this art developed an astonishing brilliance in illuminated manuscripts. The moslem religion's ban on representation of the saints, which might become the object of a cult, did not mean a rejection of all figurative art.

The Koran, in any case, makes no such ban, but limits itself to a condemnation of the worship of graven images, basing itself on the second and third commandments of the Decalogue (Exodus 20, i-iv). The Hadith, the sayings attributed to the Prophet and set down between the 7th and the late 9th centuries, are however more explicit in considering the making of images a crime. But this concerns above all graven images, statues, which "cast a shadow". It is these that might become idols and lead to a return to polytheism.

In practice, the moslem theologians' relative tolerance allowed secular painting to flourish. We have seen examples of this in the little palace of Kasr Amra with its baths, from the Umayyad period, where there is no lack of representation of animal and human forms, and where naked men and women are shown bathing.

But it was with the art of the manuscript and its miniatures that a particularly interesting pictorial art form developed, though the examples that have come down to us are, alas, rare enough. The Arab manuscript illustrators drew their inspiration directly from the illustrated Graeco-Latin works being copied and translated: the works of poets and historians, and also scientific works.

Following on from this, the original works of Arab writers were endowed with their own embellishment of miniatures. And in the 13th century, especially in Iraq (Mossul and Bagdad) and in Syria, one may find magnificent highly-coloured works combining the gold background of Byzantine work, the lively polychrome of antique manuscripts, and perhaps also the influence of pre-Islamic Persian art which had produced works of an equally exceptional splendour.

The great south door of the Abbassid palace, Bagdad, dating from the beginning of the 13th century. Here the decorative technique of chiselled brickwork achieves a remarkable level of refinement.

Bottom:

A sumptuous Arabic manuscript from Bagdad, and dating from 1287: "The Epistles of the Pure Believers", written in the 10th century and of Shiite inspiration. The two frontispiece pages represent the authors with scribes (Suleymaniye Museum, Istanbul).

The palace of the Abbassids, Bagdad, the work of the caliph Nasir al-Din Allah (1180-1225), with its double arcade and "royal" iwan in the manner of the Sassanid palaces, is built entirely in brick.

Top left:
Mosaic decoration on gold ground in Baybars' mausoleum, Zahiriyah Madrasa, Damascus. Dating from 1279, it was probably produced by Byzantine mosaicists brought back from the Egyptian sultan's victorious campaign in Anatolia. Here again the theme of paradise, with palaces and greenery.

From northern Iraq or Syria, this manuscript of the "De Materia Medica" of Dioscorides, dating from 1229, is an adaptation of the Byzantine manuscript. Dioscorides and his pupil are shown in Arab robes and turbans, but stand out against a gold ground in the Byzantine fashion (Top Kapi Library).

Detail of frontispiece page of a "Book of Songs", 1218, from the Mossul region. A king, treated full face as was proper for a sovereign, is shown surrounded by his courtiers. The style is influenced by Iranian Sassanid works.

Solon and his students, from an early 13th century manuscript. It is an illustration to "Best Sayings and Most Precious Dictums" by the writer al-Mubashshir (Top Kapi Library, Istanbul).

The Mamluks of Cairo

Facade of the Qalawun Mausoleum and its high minaret. A rigorous design making use of abutments. Built between 1284 and 1294 in Cairo on the main street of the Mamluk capital, the building mixes Islamic currents with the Gothic style brought from the Holy Land.

Detail of the above facade. Mullioned windows with a tracery in stone and colonnettes. Below the windows, a fine band of lettering.

Egypt had already in the past fallen into the hands of an undisciplined soldiery when Badr Gamali's Armenian troops had taken the Fatimid caliph of Cairo under their guardianship. Now, with the Mamluks, foreigners from the mercenary army were to hold power in the country for two and a half centuries altogether. But this "dynasty of slaves" that lasted in Egypt from 1250 to 1517 was also a period of exceptional splendour.

How did it come about that Circassians, Turks and Mongols, Armenians, Byzantine Greeks and Kurds belonging to an army of foreign mercenaries should take control of the state in an Egypt which was, at the time, the greatest Moslem power? At the time of the Fatimid dynasty's collapse and the troubles that accompanied it, then with the rise of the Ayyubid dynasty, the armed forces coming from all the corners of the earth in the pay of the caliph—as the Turks had been in Bagdad under the great Abbassids—had increasingly taken on the role of arbitrators in unstable situations. At the first opportunity they seized power on their own behalf.

We regard them as slaves, a term that translates well enough the word "Mamluk", for these mercenaries belonged to their chief and owned nothing but their arms. It was a veritable foreign legion that produced, in this period, a powerful dynasty of slave-sultans. And as one may imagine, this dynasty was riddled with bloody intrigues, fratricidal strug-

gles, assassinations, executions and torture, incarcerations and palace revolts. Yet it shone with an unbridled splendour. These slave-kings, for the most part, showed themselves to be remarkable administrators, skilful politicians, and as masters of Arab Egypt were endowed with a rare sense of grandeur and generosity.

Octagonal lantern supporting the cupola over the tomb of the Mamluk sultan Malik Mansur Qalawun, who died in 1290. Powerful granite columns alternate two to one with square pillars. Wooden stalactites make the connection between the octagon and the circular base of the cupola.

An Imperial Policy

The real intelligence of the Mamluks lay in their having made of Egypt an "Islamic kingdom". In 1258, the Abbassid caliphate at Bagdad disappeared, the Mongols having assassinated Mustasin, last caliph of the dynasty; the family's descendents fled to Egypt. Baybars re-established the caliphate, henceforth to be essentially a religious title, and Cairo, once the capital of the Shiite Fatimids, thus became the heart of the Sunnite Moslem world.

The Mamluks' policy was first of all to force the Christians out of Palestine, and with the seizure of St. John of Acre in 1291 they effectively put an end to their presence there. They then stopped the Mongols, checking every one of their attempts to establish themselves west of the Euphrates. Having established the authority of the caliph to their own

Marble decoration of a soberly elegant pattern in the Baybars II Mausoleum, Cairo, built in 1306.

Facing page:
Cupola of the mosque built by Mohammed al-Nasir in 1335 in the citadel of Cairo. The lantern with its triple windows is beautifully connected to the cupola by means of wooden stalactites, recently restored.

profit, they established a stable and unified region including Egypt as far as Nubia, Syria up to the Anatolian frontier, Arabia and the Yemen. They thus reigned simultaneously over Jerusalem, Medina and Mecca, the three holy places of Islam.

Under the Mamluks, Egypt was thus first among the Arab states from the mid-thirteenth century to the beginning of the sixteenth. They developed an original civilisation and did not, as did the Ottomans who followed them, import art forms from outside Egypt itself. Like the Abbassid empire before it, the Egypt of the Mamluks was a melting-pot of the most varied populations and tribes, cultures and ways of life, under the unifying thread of Koranic law and the Arabic language.

During this period, the wealth and luxury of Cairo was admired throughout the world. As trade developed on an international scale between Arabs and crusaders in the 13th century, while the Venetians opened trading posts in Damascus and Aleppo, the Mamluks turned Cairo into the "metropolis of the universe and garden of the world" as the historian Ibn Khaldun put it in the 14th century. For the trade between east and west under the control of the Mamluk imperial power enabled them to raise themselves to first rank among the nations of the Mediterranean.

The empire was organised along military lines. A rigorous system of promotion was set up for all governors' posts. These governors were flanked by generals directly responsible to the sultan. The administration, extremely powerful, in the tradition long since established in Egypt, was placed under a hierarchical system like that of the army itself. The post office and the tax system were also managed along military lines.

The tomb of Baybars II occupies a very sober square hall, the ceiling decorated with stone stalactites.

In the field of art, the Mamluk period is characterised by a burgeoning output of brilliant creations which reached a very high level of attainment. Architecture in particular reached a perfection that has rarely been equalled. And yet these works, contemporary with the Gothic cathedrals of Europe, remain largely misunderstood. Many specialists prefer older works and seem not to have considered them attentively. Such terms as "overloaded", "exuberant decoration", "charming ornamentation" repeated in certain writings are perplexing to anyone who knows and loves this powerful art, an art which is sometimes awe-inspiring. The quality of the construction in fine, regular dressed stone with a perfect stereotomy, the beauty of the always sober materials chosen, never flashy or loud, the sense of spareness in the walls allied to a rigorous precision of detail, the finesse of a generally sparing decoration, makes of this art an authoritative model of stylistic originality.

The layout, though sometimes complex, is always logical, with a vigorous articulation and always using clearly distinct elements: great iwans with tierce-point vaulting, at first in brick and later in cut stone, giving onto huge interior courtyards with polychrome pavements; tombs under high cupolas; madrasas with wide spaces covered here with magnificent raftered and panelled ceilings, there with stone vaulting; polygonal minarets with galleries supported by stalactites.

Courtyard of Mohammed al-Nasir's mosque, in the citadel of Cairo: one can see, in the prayer hall, the four heavier columns supporting the lantern cupola.

Top:
The double lateral portico of the Mohammed al-Nasir mosque, Cairo: above the columns, two tiers of arches, as in the Umayyad mosque in Damascus.

This is an architecture which has found solutions to its technical problems that are highly authentic and extremely resistant, as witness the good state of preservation in which most of these buildings have survived the vicissitudes of five to seven centuries' existence.

Side by side in this architecture we find the lessons of Armenia and Byzantium brought by Syrian engineers in the Fatimid period, formulae derived from the building work of the Franks in the Holy Land, and Islamic traditions in the use of space and geometric decoration.

Before recounting the series of sumptuous Mamluk buildings that adorn Cairo, we should first look at the tomb of Baybars, one of the first sultans of the dynasty, in the Zahiriye Madrasa at Damascus. Unendingly at war with the crusaders, Baybars adopted Syria as his centre of activity, seizing Caesaraea and Antioch in turn. His tomb, with its marble veneers, its friezes, its mosaic tympanums decorated with trees and palaces on a gold ground in the Byzantine manner, reminds one of the decoration of the Great Mosque of the Umayyads and shows the survival of Byzantine techniques in the Arab world. Perhaps the craftsmen who worked on it were Greek prisoners brought back from the victorious campaign in Anatolia...

The Tomb of Qalawun

Among the great Mamluk works in Cairo, we must mention in first place the mausoleum and madrasa of Malik Mansur Qalawun, a sultan of Turkish origin who died in 1290 at the age of 70. This complex, built in the centre of the ancient capital, was constructed between 1284 and 1294. Its long, high facade faces onto the city's main street where it replaced parts of the old Fatimid palaces.

Two buildings are as it were juxtaposed within the complex: the tomb itself and the mosque-madrasa built for the funerary rites. The two are

Built in 1334, the Bishtak Palace, Cairo, is one of the few secular buildings of the Mamluk period still standing. Above the side aisles are galleries, like the triforium of a Gothic church.

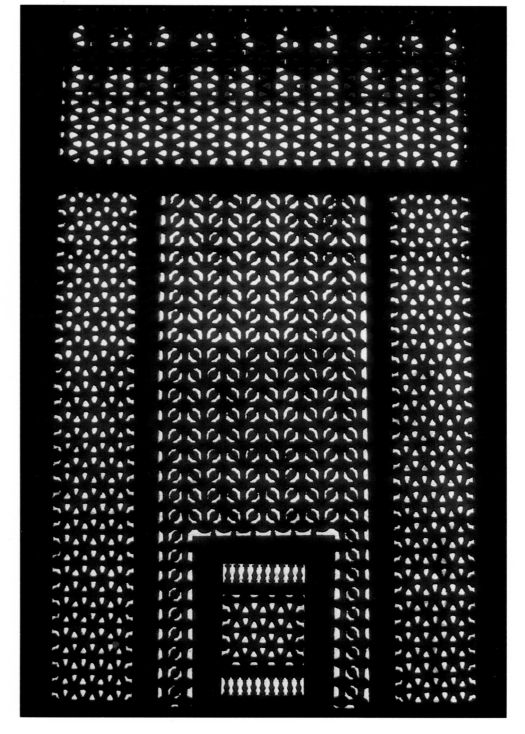

Detail of the window with wooden tracery, or mucharabieh, from the Bishtak Palace, Cairo.

The luxuriant polychromed wood stalactites of the cupola in Sultan Hassan's Tomb, Cairo.

Two details from the decoration of the Sultan Hassan Madrasa, Cairo: an inscription on a doorjamb, and arch mouldings in marble veneer.

separated by a long dark corridor into which a portal leads directly from the street. As one enters the Qalawun complex, the tomb lies to one's right, where a door leads into a vestibule before one reaches the hall of the mausoleum proper. This hall, on an almost square plan, presents eight powerful pillars supporting pointed arches, from which the octagon of a high cupola rises. Four of these supports are huge monolithic columns of pink granite, probably re-cycled from antique buildings,

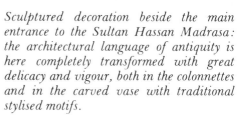

Sculptured decoration beside the main entrance to the Sultan Hassan Madrasa: the architectural language of antiquity is here completely transformed with great delicacy and vigour, both in the colonnettes and in the carved vase with traditional stylised motifs.

Detail of the fine bronze door to the Sultan Hassan Madrasa: a magnificent but unaffected work of geometric design.

while the other four are solid square pillars. Under the tremendous canopy, the tomb lies along the axis between the entrance and the lovely niche of an oriented mihrab which combines with great delicacy the techniques of marble marquetry, mosaic and inlaid precious metals. The interior walls of the high drum supporting the cupola itself have a stucco decoration comparable to certain Fatimid and even Tulunid works. The eight mullioned windows, each of two lights with a small round "œil de bœuf" above, are reminiscent of Gothic architecture, an influence one may equally see in the vertical arrangement of the facade with the stone tracery of its windows divided by colonnettes and set

The courtyard at the heart of the Sultan Hassan Madrasa, with its four majestic iwans. Built in Cairo between 1356 and 1363, it constitutes the masterpiece of Mamluk architecture. The archways of the iwans are over 26 metres (85 feet) high. In the centre, the ablution fountain, and in the right foreground the rostrum where the muezzin reproduces the imam's gestures of prayer.

The mihrab of the Sultan Hassan is a marvellous play of contrasting marbles in a sober, calm structure.

The immense vaulted doorway of the Sultan Hassan Madrasa in Cairo, with its honeycomb of stalactites. Above it is a deep overhanging cornice, also with stalactites. To the left, the vertical rows of windows in the Koranic school, separated by abutments.

between projecting abutments. And in the hall of the mausoleum one may perhaps see an allusion to the Dome of the Rock.

The madrasa lies to the south, on one's left as one enters the corridor, and is designed in the Iranian tradition with a huge courtyard bordered on three sides by iwans while the fourth side, forming the prayer hall, is divided into three aisles by arcades running at right angles to the qibla.

Some emphasis should be given to a characteristic aspect of most of the urban complexes of the Mamluk period: their integration into an already existing urban environment, with just one facade on the street and their other three sides directly up against the surrounding buildings. This often entails a somewhat tortuous layout with surprising disconnections, twists and turns, which make up half the charm of this powerful and sober art in which, with a haughty grandeur, a harmonious marriage is made between the most diverse artistic currents of the world of Islam and formulae introduced into the Holy Land by the Franks.

On a plan that relates to that of the funerary complex of Qalawun, the ensemble of the tomb and madrasa-monastery of the sultan Baybars II al-Jashnakir was built in 1306. Here too one finds a corridor leading to the mausoleum and madrasa, the madrasa laid out in the classic Persian cruciform style with four iwans. But here the corridor, preceded by a gateway and entrance hall, gives access to a complex where one element lies behind the other, the tomb having one narrow facade onto the street and the madrasa beyond being completely out of sight among the surrounding buildings. In this architecture one sees how pride of place has been given to the interior spaces.

The tomb chamber is a square hall with a stonework cupola resting on pendentives of fine stalactites. In it one can see a tendency to translate forms into geometric shapes; the same tendency is characteristic of the decorated windows and niches in the courtyard. Again in the treatment of the lattice windows with coloured glass panes that light the mausoleum one is brought back to a play of hexagons that gives a visual continuity with the stalactites, from which all trace of the spherical forms of Persian mukarnas has disappeared.

The Works of Mohammed al-Nasir

Qalawun's son and successor in the Mamluk dynasty, the sultan Mohammed al-Nasir, had a truly epic career, like several other sovereigns of his time: he came to the sultans' throne at the age of ten and was deposed in 1294 before he had reigned a full year. Four years later he had returned to power, but was once again deposed at the age of twenty-four; persisting, he regained the throne at twenty-five and then maintained himself in power for thirty-three years of uninterrupted rule until his death in 1341.

His madrasa-mausoleum, near Qalawun's complex, has a great door onto the street whose history is exemplary of the Mamluks' attitudes towards their enemies the crusaders. One sees here a tympanum wholly Gothic in style, and multiple arches resting on small columns with elaborate capitals. It is, quite simply, the doorway of the cathedral of St. John of Acre, completely dismantled after the seizure of the city in 1291 by al-Achraf, Qalawun's other son. Transported stone by stone to Cairo as a trophy of war, but with all the care and respect due to an architectural work of high quality, it was reconstructed between 1296 and 1303 at the entrance to the mausoleum of Mohammed al-Nasir, where one may still admire it to this day.

But the sultan's most important work remains the mosque he had built at the end of his reign, in 1335, within the walled city of Cairo built long before by Saladin. Seen from outside, this mosque has an austere look with its bare walls, its high, deeply recessed doorway hung with stalactites and its single row of small windows all around the building at

Bottom:
Prayer hall of the Barkuk mosque, Cairo: within the sober architecture of this 1389 structure, a luxuriant ceiling in wood with gilded decoration.

Detail of the entrance door to the Barkuk mosque, Cairo, showing the delicacy of the bronze fretwork.

the top of the outer wall. But inside lies a huge square courtyard, bordered on three sides by double porticos and on the fourth by a hypostyle prayer hall. The hall's supports are mainly re-used columns, these surmounted by arcades on which stands a second range of smaller arches, two to each arch below as in the Umayyad mosque at Damascus. These pointed arches with their alternating arch-stones in contrasting colour run parallel to the qibla. The mihrab itself bears a high cupola on wooden pendentives decorated with stalactites, which has recently, and very tastefully, been restored.

The Majesty of the Sultan Hassan

It is to Malik Nasir Hassan, grandson of Qalawun and son of Mohammed al-Nasir, that we owe the most extraordinary masterpiece of the Mamluk dynasty in Cairo: this is the Madrasa of Sultan Hassan, also known as "the Sumptuous".

The life of this man too is representative of those dramatic careers in which the epoque was so rich: coming to the throne at twelve years of age, he was deposed at sixteen; then again seized power three years later, but ruled for only seven years, for he was finally assassinated at the age of twenty-six in 1361.

East door of the Barkukiyah, the mausoleum of Barkuk, built between 1399 and 1410 in the Caliphs' Cemetery, Cairo.

One of the stone cupolas of the Barkukiyah, above the building's eastern mausoleum. Its carved decoration of chevrons, and the powerfully moulded sloping shoulders of its pendentives, make it one of the most original works of the Mamluk period.

The madrasa he founded, and which was erected between 1356 and 1363, is the work of a Syrian architect who brought together the lessons of Persia and the techniques of the Mamluk age. This colossal monument, which includes the sovereign's tomb and a funerary madrasa, measures 150 metres by 70 (160 yards by 75). Built outside the Fatimid city walls of Cairo, at the foot of Saladin's stronghold, this monument, unlike his predecessor's, has not been fitted into an already standing urban tissue, but on the contrary stands apart, an imposing, solitary building. It abuts no pre-existent structure and offers proud, free facades on all fronts. Its considerable proportions take on yet greater vigour from its majestic isolation.

It is designed within an irregular but roughly rectangular area. To the

north is the entrance, at the centre the cruciform madrasa with its court-yard bordered by enormous iwans with tierce-point arches, and to the south lies the square mausoleum surmounted by a high cupola and flanked by two minarets. The outer walls of the madrasa of Sultan Hassan stand 30 metres (100 feet) high and are topped by an imposing overhanging cornice hung with stalactites. This proud silhouette, broken only by occasional vertical ranges of windows between powerful abutments, has all the appearance of a "fortress of the faith".

Built throughout in fine, regular dressed stone and with remarkably little decoration, the madrasa draws yet greater power from its simplicity. But it is within the central courtyard that the Sultan Hassan reveals in full its austere beauty. The four arches of the immense iwans

The square courtyard of the Barkukiyah, with its portico flanked by two superb minarets, their galleries supported by stalactite corbels. In the centre, the ablution fountain.

85

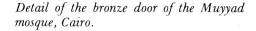

Detail of the bronze door of the Muyyad mosque, Cairo.

Top left:
The Muyyad mosque, Cairo, dating from 1415, repeats the formula of chevron-carved dome.

Above right:
The fine prayer hall of the Muyyad mosque, light and airy. The qibla wall is entirely faced in marble veneer, replying to the elegance of the ceiling's gilded wood panels supported by two rows of octagonal pillars. In the centre the minbar, from where the imam addresses his audience from the top of the steps to the seat which represents the Prophet's very simple throne at Medina.

surround an octagonal ablution fountain. And while the decoration is sparing throughout the courtyard, limited to the scalloped arches of the doorways and an alternating pattern of light and reddish-brown stone, the great southern iwan, on the contrary, containing the mihrab, is superbly faced in polychrome marbles which sparkle in the shadow of its vault. And lastly, in the square funerary hall, with the cupola above stretching across a diameter of 22 metres (24 yards) and supported on stalactites of gilded and painted wood, here is concentrated all the richness of a glowing decoration.

The Cemetery of the Caliphs

To the east of Cairo, at the desert's edge, stands an immense necropolis where the Circassian caliphs who took the Mamluk throne from 1382 onwards came to build their mausoleums. In this city of the dead one can see the distant influence of the Pharaonic necropoles: the tombs, surrounded by walls, resemble—as Ibn Battutah has said—real houses, in the same way as the mastabas of ancient Egypt were translations in stone of the cob-walled houses of the living.

This imposing and eternal appearance of the city of the dead, which so enraptured the first western visitors to enter Cairo, visitors who said the Saracens' tombs were more reminiscent of a city than of a cemetery, finds its finest expression in the Mausoleum of Barkuk. Also called the Barkukiyah, this complex is the monumental work of a sultan who came to power only at the age of forty-six, was deposed at fifty-three, and regained the throne less than a year later to keep it for a further ten years, until his death at the age of sixty-three.

The mosque-madrasa of Barkuk was constructed with a funerary purpose, on a rigorously square plan 73 metres (80 yards) on each side, the two entrances its only projecting elements. Inside, a huge courtyard 40 metres (44 yards) square, surrounded by porticos, gives onto a hypostyle hall whose roof is a series of small cupolas supported by octagonal pillars with tall stilted arches.

The symmetrical structure also includes at its northern corners two very elegant minarets 50 metres (165 feet) high, while the prayer hall is flanked at each end by an imposing cupola in stone, 35 metres (115 feet) high, occupying the corners of the south front. These cupolas are decorated with an original carving on the outside of the dome's shell, a model which was to be taken up in many works of that dynasty. In the interior, they show stalactite pendentives of the most skilful masonrywork.

The creator of this majestic building, constructed between 1399 and 1410, was an architect by the name of Cherkis al-Haranbuli. He developed a powerful style combining a free use of techniques and media and a great sincerity of form, always simple. The decoration is restricted to the minarets, the cupolas and the frieze of merlons which top the courtyard and exterior walls and lighten their effect.

This necropolis, the Cemetery of the Caliphs, was enriched during the Mamluk dynasty by a whole series of mausoleums in which a refined art was developed sacrificing monumental scale only to gain in elegance. There was increasing recourse to asymmetrical compositions, skilfully articulated, where such elements as gateways, courtyard, domed funerary hall and minaret are combined in ever-renewed and fresh arrangements.

These characteristics can be found in the mausoleum of Qaitbay dating from 1474, or again in that of the sultan Kurkmas, built in 1507, shortly before the fall of the Mamluks in the face of the Turkish Ottoman armies. The splendour of this dynasty collapsed abruptly with the discovery, in 1498, of the sea route from Europe to India round the Cape. The circumnavigation of Africa ruined Egypt, through which until then all trade from the Far East had passed. This international trade had earned the Mamluks—like the pre-Islamic Arabs before them—the wealth that had upheld their militarily-organised power.

Detail of the facade of the al-Ghuri Madrasa. Decoration became richer in the later Mamluk works.

Top:
Funerary mosque of the sultan al-Ghuri, Cairo, built in 1507—the facade on the street, opposite the same sovereign's madrasa.

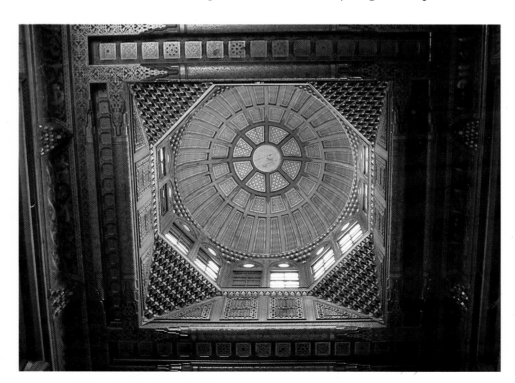

Wooden lantern cupola above the main hall of the sultan al-Ghuri's Madrasa, Cairo.

The Islamic Heritage

It is to the development of the Koranic school, the madrasa, and its eventual distribution throughout the Islamic world of the middle ages that one must attribute the elevated level of culture from the 10th century on. Public teaching benefitted, and at least half the male population of the larger urban centres knew how to read and write in the Arab Moslem world. In particular many translations were made of scientific works from antiquity: Archimedes, Euclid, Ptolemy, Hero of Alexandria and Galen could be read in Arabic. And in return, by the twelfth century one could count some three hundred Arabic works translated into Latin for the benefit of Western scientists of the day. For Arab scientists had furthered the researches of the Greeks and Romans, deepening their methodology and experimental techniques.

In the fields of astronomy, physics, mathematics, chemistry, the natural sciences and medicine, the Arab scientists shone. These were the creators of algebraic calculus, of sine and cosine tables; they established the bases of spherical trigonometry thanks to which astronomy was able to make great leaps forward. They laid the foundations, in a real sense, of chemistry, distilling alcohol and sulphuric acid and determining the properties of a number of substances. These discoveries they were able to apply to pharmacy and medical science. Progress was made in the field of surgery. Thus was the Arab civilisation the educator of the Western world on the eve of the Renaissance.

In speaking of these discoveries, special mention must be made of the introduction of such instruments as the astrolabe, a calculating instrument from which one could measure the altitude above the horizon of any heavenly body. Navigation progressed thanks also to the introduction of the compass, already known in China. And the diffusion of science was only possible with the introduction of paper, also originally from China but which the Arabs brought to the Middle East and manufactured there from an early date.

Numerous were the Arab thinkers, philosophers and historians who enriched the heritage of mankind. In the time of the Mamluks, for example, Ibn Khaldun, born in 1334 and who died in Cairo in 1406, was at once philosopher, geographer, historian, ethnographer, traveller and diplomat. He was the founder of sociology. And this spirit of rationalism was an all-embracing spirit which brought together a synthesis of all the memory of mankind.

Many other names worthy of mention contributed their piece to the monument of civilisation. Too often, the fact that they were Arab has meant the relegation of their names to oblivion.

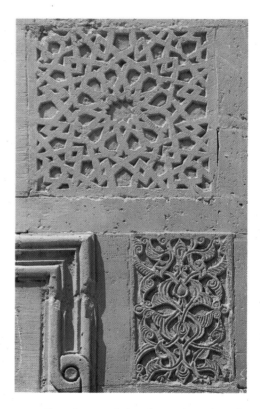

Detail of Mamluk decoration in the Caliphs' Cemetery, Cairo.

Tomb of the sultan Kurkmas, dating from 1507, in the Caliphs' Cemetery, Cairo. The decoration is perhaps overdone, but the forms in late Mamluk works retain all their power. Cupolas in particular achieve greater lightness, echoed in the soaring minarets.

Moroccan Splendours

Gold coin of the Almoravid dynasty, 11th or 12th century. Morocco lay at the end of the trans-Sahara trail carrying a trade in gold and black African slaves (Batha Museum, Fez).

Facing page:
An astrolabe, one of the essential navigational instruments of the middle ages. Invented in the days of antiquity, this calculator composed of eccentric discs made it possible to measure the altitude of a star above the horizon. The Arabs improved considerably the technology of these astrolabes; this one may date back to the 12th century, and measures 24.2 centimetres (9 ½ inches) across (Batha Museum, Fez).

At the far western end of the Arab world, the development of Islam followed an original path which soon separated it from the destinies of the great classical dynasties. The Arab armies of the Umayyads had already reached the Atlantic in 682, and 710 marked the completion of the conquest of Barbary; but confrontation continued for many years between Arabs and Berbers, giving birth to a series of independent and antagonistic dynasties and small kingdoms.

Opposition to Sunnite orthodoxy was marked by the spread of the Kharijite doctrine among the berbers from 760 onwards, inspired by Alid beliefs. At first it was a dissident Arab dynasty, that of the Idrissids, founded by Idris I, a descendent of Ali, which laid the foundations of an independent kingdom in Morocco. Idris II built Fez in 807 and made it his capital. These kings remained in power until their defeat by the Fatimids of Ifriqiyah in the early 10th century.

After them came the Almoravid dynasty, of Berber origin and from the south, of an ethically strict religious persuasion, who established their rule from 1055 on. The Almoravids founded the city of Marrakesh and launched holy wars both against the Negro peoples of the south—land of gold and of slaves—and against the mountain chieftains. They eventually occupied the whole of the Maghreb. These Berber Moslems, despite their hostility to the Arab invaders, nevertheless spoke the language of the Koran. As the Christian forces advanced through Spain, forcing ahead the Reconquista, the Almoravids brought military aid to the Moslem forces in Spain and defeated the Spanish troops at Zalacca in 1086.

The Almohads, southerners too, founded a Berber dynasty in 1130 and in 1145 carried a decisive victory against the Almoravids, then launched in turn a campaign of conquest against Moslem Spain, which they took in 1163. Then in 1195 at the battle of Alarcos they defeated the Spanish Christians.

From there, there followed a fragmentation, with a Berber dynasty, the Merinids, ruling in Fez from 1238, and the Nasrids, Arab lords of Spain, established in their palaces in Granada during the last centuries of the Moslem presence in Andalusia. With the Saladins in 1532 it was an Arab dynasty that checked the ambitions of the Portuguese over Morocco. And again the Alawites, who came to the throne in 1659 and restored the threatened unity of the country, were also of Arab origin.

Originality in Decoration

In the artistic field, all of Morocco and the Maghreb shows, from the time of the creation of Qayrawan and of Cordoba, a traditionalist character as far as layout and the organisation of space is concerned.

This conservative architecture of the mosques, with their courtyards and hypostyles, is however enhanced by an exceptional decorative sensibility from the time of the Merinids onwards. The Merinids unhesitatingly endowed madrasas and palaces alike with a most luxuriant decoration, making use of a combination of media such as chiselled stucco work, polychrome tiles, marble veneer and delicate woodwork set off by elaborately worked bronze.

It is true that this Merinid style is a close parallel to that developing in Spain under the Nasrids of Granada. It is a refined art, sensual, voluptuous, with a splendour that vigorously rejects the austerity previously imposed by the Berber kings of the puritan Almoravid and Almohad dynasties. There is also perhaps a certain decadence expressed in the intricacy of the tiny polychromed plaster stalactites or in the abundance of chiselled arabesques.

The use of multifoil arches and heavily-decorated lattice-work cupolas finds a counterbalance in the massive solidity of the square minarets and the powerful strength of the fortified walls around the cities.

It is nevertheless the case that the Moslem west has forged its own artistic language which is not to be confused with any other. One can read in it a high culture, a refined civilisation on which the Spanish kings

Detail of the decoration in the al-Attarine Madrasa, built between 1323 and 1325 in Fez during the Merinid dynasty: a band of lettering cut in plaster above a second such band in ceramic tiles and, below, a geometric mosaic of coloured ceramic tiles.

Interior courtyard of the Qayrawan mosque in Fez, founded in the 10th century but renovated and enlarged several times, particularly in 1135 under the Almoravids.

Standing out against the Atlas mountain chain, the gardens and summerhouses of the Menara, Marrakesh, constructed in the 12th century under the Almohads.

of the Renaissance were to draw, contracting the construction of their own palaces and the decoration of their churches to the mudejars. This, however, is another story, one to which we shall return in our future book, "The World of Spain".

A Fascinating Path

So it is on the shores of the Atlantic, on the borders of black Africa, that the extraordinary adventure of the Arab people reaches its limits. The chronicle of these men of the Middle East who, even before the birth of Christ, had ventured beyond their peninsula, a land largely of desert apart from the rich cultivation of aromatics in the Yemen and the Hadramaut, to found their desert gateways between East and West.

Following the preaching of Mohammed, under the impulse of their ardent monotheistic Islamic faith, they launched their attack on the ancient empires. Their conquering waves, giving them mastery over one of the vastest territories ever united under one power, allowed them to forge their own artistic language and their own civilisation.

Fountain in the entrance hall of the Mulay Ishmail mausoleum, Meknes, built in the early 18th century. Throughout moslem architecture, water plays an eminent part, and here its murmur under echoing vaults gives an impression of coolness.

Above right:
Interior of the Ben Saadian tombs at Marrakesh, from the first half of the 16th century: a delicate and refined art which relates to the Nasrid palace at Granada.

And if they made use of the Hellenistic style in the days of Petra, of Roman styles in Palmyra, Romano-Parthian in Hatra, Byzantine in Jerusalem and Damascus, they did not delay in elaborating their own particular forms, especially as regards the mosque, a new function which called for the creation of a new kind of building. These hypostyles with their courtyards are an authentically Moslem invention, to which were later added the formulae of iwans, taken from Sassanid Persia.

As much on the artistic as the cultural level, the Arab world gave birth to an inheritance of a richness and quality that demands our admiration. Their learned men, mathematicians, chemists, astronomers and doctors, as much as their poets, philosophers, thinkers and mystics, have brought to humanity, with the Arab legacy, one of the major contributions to civilisation.

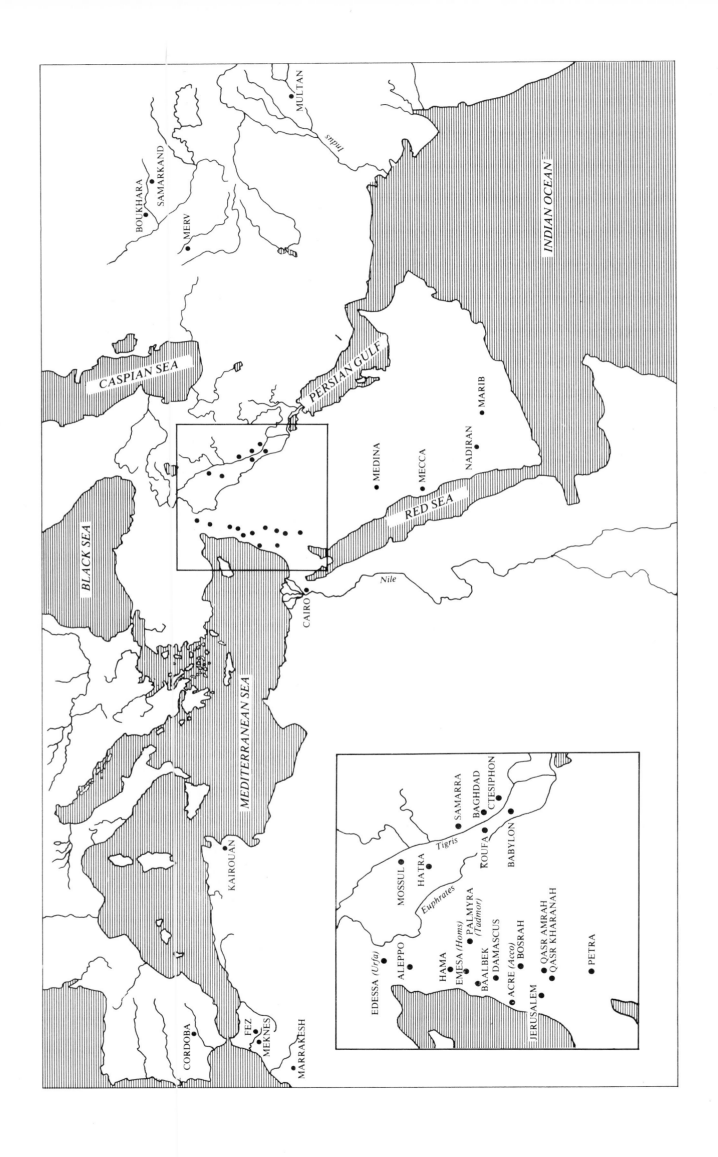

BOUKHARA

SAMARKAND

MERV

MULTAN

Indus

CASPIAN SEA

PERSIAN GULF

MARIB

NADIRAN

MEDINA

MECCA

RED SEA

BLACK SEA

INDIAN OCEAN

Nile

CAIRO

MEDITERRANEAN SEA

KAIROUAN

FEZ

MEKNES

CORDOBA

MARRAKESH

EDESSA (*Urfa*)

ALEPPO

HAMA

EMESA (*Homs*)

BAALBEK

DAMASCUS

ACRE (*Acco*)

BOSRAH

JERUSALEM

MOSSUL

HATRA

Euphrates

PALMYRA (*Tadmor*)

Tigris

SAMARRA

BAGHDAD

CTESIPHON

KOUFA

BABYLON

QASR AMRAH

QASR KHARANAH

PETRA